Spiritual Physics

Another Generation's View of the Work of
G. I. Gurdjieff

Compiled and edited by
John Anderson and Marshall May

A practical guide to the science of being known as
The Fourth Way

JERRY BREWSTER

SPIRITUAL PHYSICS

Another Generations' View of the Work of G. I. Gurdjieff

Compiled and edited by
John Anderson and Marshall May

A practical guide to the science of being known as
The Fourth Way

Edition 5

PUBLISHING

JAMM Publications
1641 Third Ave. #31DE
New York, NY 10128
917-562-5205
954- 205-9652

Fifth Edition
Printed in the United States of America

Library of Congress Cataloging-in-Publication Data
ISBN 978-1-503-24660-7
TXu 1-884-382
October 1, 2013

CONTENTS

v

vii

WARNING

All men are dead, except those who know.

All those who know are dead, except those who practice.

All those who practice are dead, except those who act.

All those who act are dead, except those who act with righteous intent.

All those who act with righteous intent are in grave danger!

Twelfth-century Egyptian Sufi

Introduction

Between the two of us we knew Jerry for over fifty years. He was both spiritual teacher and essence friend. It is difficult to sum up in a few words our years with a man who had taken himself from the humblest of beginnings to a man of being. Jerry followed the teachings of G. I. Gurdjieff, better known today as the Fourth Way. He devoted over fifty years of his life to the practice and teaching of what has become known as the Work and made great efforts to expand the understanding of it. Jerry's view of the Work was very scientific. He struggled to pass on the principles, tasks, and ideas of the work experience to his pupils.

Those of you who knew Jerry will be familiar with his language. For those who didn't, be very careful in trying to understand this unique language, especially where it involves his further research into understanding the Enneagram.

In the summer of 2006 several of his students invited him to their homes and taped sessions of questions and answers with him. He did sixteen of these sessions, and they cover decades of study and work. In our edit, we changed the sequence of these and reordered them into chapters. It was Jerry's stated intention to publish this material to help future group leaders and other seekers and their successors and to aid in their movement to the next rung.

As you start to read these questions and answers you will become increasingly aware of references to Jerry's own personal understanding of the Enneagram and a special relationship with the energy called hydrogen 24. To Jerry's students and others who worked with him over the years, this will be familiar ground, but for those without this familiarity we have included two special Chapters, 13 and 14, taken from various talks he gave on the subjects. We would like to make it clear that these offer only a rudimentary view of Jerry's new understanding of the Enneagram and the energy called hydrogen 24, as he came to see it.

John Anderson and Marshall May

When P. D. Ouspensky was asked if he intended to publish his lectures, he answered: "What is the use? The most important is not the lectures, but the questions and answers."

WITH APPRECIATION:

We wish to express our appreciation to everyone who contributed to this process, especially Gary Strum who gave us the benefit of his expertise in editing and helped in every way, even when we didn't take his advice. Thanks also to Adriana Tanganelli-Williams for artwork of the Enneagram, and to Andy De Santis for his help in editing some of it, as well as Steve Adams for his grammatical assistance. Special thanks are also due to the group who questioned Jerry and taped the meetings, and also the very many throughout the Brewster groups who helped transcribe the tapes into digital form. Thanks are due to Bill Tidwell, Carl Lehman-Haupt, and David Appelbaum for their comments, criticism, and encouragement, and a special prize for patience to Barbara May who put up with a lot.

Editor's note:

In addition to the meetings which are the subject of this book, over the years John Anderson taped many of Jerry's talks, lunches, meetings, and lectures from the mid-1980s until his death. We have selected some of these words of wisdom as part of preparatory notes and as lead-ins to the chapters to recognize Jerry's great interest in sacred stories.

PREPARATORY NOTES
by Jerry Brewster

Someone once asked Gurdjieff, "From what does the Way start?" "The chief difficulty in understanding the idea of the Way," said G., "consists in the fact that people usually think that the Way starts on the same level on which life is going. This is quite wrong. The Way begins on another, much higher, level." He also said: "The moment when the man who is looking for the way meets a man who knows the way is called the first threshold or the first step. From this first threshold the stairway begins. Between 'life' and the 'Way' lies the 'stairway.'" Yet, this Work is not ultimately to depend on Gurdjieff or Mme. de Salzmann or some guru or master to bring you the energy or do the work for you. We must understand how very important this first triad of Work is: self-observation, self-remembering, seeing ourselves, and preparing in ourselves an attention that can work along real lines of real Work. To a group that is working on first conscious shock remembering oneself in the first triad of the Enneagram is the representative of self-remembering. In the second triad it would be true self-remembering, the sensation of I to the feeling of I; this is quiet mind receiving impressions for the sake of 'unity. Everything comes down to the unification of the centers, what Gurdjieff called a permanent I, which comes out of the unification of centers.

When we first come to the Work we're placed in a preparatory group because preparation is necessary before one is given work to unify the centers. Gurdjieff brought out the idea that one may have a wish, but not be able to struggle. It is very important "to be able to. The first triad, the preparatory work between life and real Work is the generation of the ability to be able to Work. Struggle is a work in itself, but it's still preparatory work. Even though it may be preparatory work, I'm still starting to develop my attention in a way that I will always use in the future. My attention has been atrophied. Not only must I learn to develop an attention, but also to divide it; and we climb the ladder the same way in the first triad as in the second. There is a phrase I came across recently that I think explains this: "Detachment, separation, unification, the three stages of attention." First to detach oneself, to be unidentified; second, separation, to actually sense part of one's body while in action. As I said earlier, in order for there to be unification, two centers are brought together at first, but eventually I must inhabit all three centers simultaneously.

This can facilitate a separation from your personality. It's not personality seeing itself, it is now an objective part observing. This is what sensation does when there are two centers present and a division of attention. Vibration of your leg will call for part of that I, and that breaks the hallucination that I'm in. One of the things that Gurdjieff said which is quoted in the journal of Bernard Metz, "One center: hallucination; two centers: half hallucination; three centers: awake."

In a way you are trying to cure an addiction to one-centeredness. It's one thing to be in a coma and another to be awake with your eyes open lying in bed. It is something else to be awake, totally in action. But we live in a coma. When you bring your attention to the moment and you awaken to that moment, you realize you've been gone; you really look and try to understand where you were when you didn't exist! Half hallucination isn't so bad; in fact, it's a very big thing. It's the same effort of attention on every level. The question is of degree. With false personality and essence, you are white-washing a burning house. If you reach the level of consciousness of Man No. 4, at that level of being you could understand that unless you achieve a crystallization of your finer vibrations, everything will be dissipated. When the house is burned down, what do you have? It went somewhere! Remember, in the universe nothing is destroyed, it just changes form. What happens to me when I die? My form changes just like the burning house. If I'm cremated, there will be smoke, cinders; gases will be released. But what's left? You bury it, right? What's left is a corpse, food for insects and bacteria.

In the food diagram, we see that there are three foods: physical food, air, and impressions. The interaction of all three will transform energy up to a certain point. Every frequency of vibration has its own value system, its own tempo, its own consciousness, and even its own body and circulation. We must begin to understand that we have a responsibility to further transform this energy. You must be able to generate it for yourself. We are playing for great stakes. Gurdjieff provides the most optimistic and positive system of ideas that I have ever come across because of what we could become! In religion, they say we are born in the image of God, but what does that mean? In the Work, Gurdjieff says, "Our higher centers are there, and are already developed." We have the "centers of God," so to speak. We have the higher vibrations within us but we can't connect with them because we live through our personality, which is at such a low vibration.

"There is a magnetism that pulls us back to our thoughts, which are usually just associations relating to the past or future. Our 'muscle of attention' has never been exercised and is very weak. In the freeing of our attention from this magnetism it's possible to 'travel' inwards . . . opening a door to new places in us that heretofore were invisible."

1

ATTENTION

1.01   Q: What is attention? How can we see and know our attention? What do we mean when we speak about the division or the expansion of attention?

JB: One of the great mysteries is, "What is my attention?" I've heard, "The attention is me." But in one of his talks Gurdjieff used the phrase "active attention." I tried to understand that, and the way I worked at it was what would the opposite be? What is a nonactive attention? What I realized is that for everybody in the world, and for me until I met the Work, our attention follows the path of least resistance. Whatever calls it, it follows. I don't have an authority in me that acts for the whole of me, no permanent I, an authority that the attention will obey. We often use the same word—attention—for lack of attention, captive attention, directed attention, divided attention, or what I call "expanded attention," which includes more than one center. Normally, the attention follows the path of least resistance and the other is an attention that's of consciousness, out of the path of least resistance. Awakening is connected with this living attention. The biggest problem we face in our ordinary, mechanical state is that our attention is invisible or imperceptible to us; we don't even know attention exists. We become whatever the attention is called to, which Gurdjieff calls "identification," actually becoming it, not just thinking it.

When we first come to the Work, everyone is given tasks which demand taking the attention out of the path of least resistance. These tasks represent an authority that my attention can relate to and result in a more collected state. We don't start with the mind because we're so identified with our thoughts; we actually become the thoughts. We can't trust the mind in our present state. Just as I dream at night and I believe the dream, when I wake up in the morning I believe I'm awake: the same delusion. Eventually, we will be able to trust the mind, if and when we learn the real energy of the mind. Same thing with the emotions. They're too powerful for me; again, I'm too identified. We usually begin with the moving center because it's the most available. I don't know my real body. I only know the body through postures and tensions. But I can learn to be aware of the vibration of sensation of the body. The sensations are always there; our body is filled with sensations, but I'm not aware of them because they're usually blocked by tensions. As I struggle with certain tasks, sensation becomes available to me, and I can use this sensation to verify the fact that my attention is taken out of the path of least resistance. For instance, I'm sensing my left leg, but next second I'm dreaming; but then I renew the effort and sense my left leg again. I'm to first remember, and then verify the effort through the use of another center. I'm actually exercising my attention. Like any muscle, it needs to be used. Our attention has been atrophied. Attention's been invisible, and I'm now making it visible. I was born with the ability to use this attention, but my "education" kept me away from that struggle. If there's no demand for awakening, it's not a task. Certain spiritual ways begin with this kind of education. Our reeducation begins when we meet a Way. Certain Tibetan Buddhist rituals include a demand for the attention to be pulled out of the path of least resistance as a way to consciousness. Certain tasks allow the attention to be seen. There has to be an expansion of the attention to include two forces; the sensation of my leg is the active force, it's really the attention. The passive force is my mechanicality, the path of least resistance. Also, there is a division of the attention: one part of the attention is mechanical and the other part is conscious.

Now I'm centered in the body, and I sense without that pull of my mechanicality. I connect with the sensation and then I try to open to the energy of my mind. The sensation could be active instead of passive in relation to my ordinary mind or personality; it could also be passive to a higher thought. I need to be open to two forces, and two centers could represent that. It could also be that I'm open to myself, and I open to you, again, expansion of the attention, the opening to two forces. All of this demands an awakening so they can reconcile and bring you to the next level. Gurdjieff said, "The higher blends with the lower in order together to actualize the middle and thus to become either higher for the preceding lower or lower for the succeeding higher."

1.02   Q: Can you talk about the relationship between attention and sensation, and what is the relationship between sensation and tension?

JB: There are many references to 'The practice of presence.' Brother Lawrence wrote a book about that, *The Practice of the Presence of God*. He said, "That in the winter, seeing a tree stripped of its leaves, and considering that within a little time, the leaves would be renewed, and after that the flowers and fruit appear, he received a high view of the Providence and Power of God, which has never since been effaced from his soul."

The Buddha gave a sutra on the setting up of mindfulness. He didn't mean mental mind. He meant being present. To paraphrase, he said, "I take in a short breath, and I'm aware of letting out a short breath. I take in a long breath, and I am aware I'm letting out a long breath." He is saying, don't manipulate the breath; don't change it; be aware of it in the body.

What we see of the moon is the reflection of the light of the sun. Our personality is the reflection of the light of our essence. Just like the sense of I that we see is a reflection. I need sensation in order to make the attention visible. I've heard it said that I am my attention. Look inside yourself and ask, "What is my attention? Where is my attention?" Making the attention visible requires certain exercises and efforts. Part of a sitting is a collecting exercise; the moving of the attention to different parts of the body can have the result of relaxation. Or, the attention can be seen by using a habit as a reminding factor: the moment I lose my attention, the habit appears! As an example, if I try not to gesticulate when I'm speaking, the moment I lose my attention, my hands move. If I'm a little bit present, I see it and it reminds me.

As I continue to sense and then lose my sense of I, I start to become aware of this movement of attention and its action becomes visible, the attention going back and forth. First, I direct the attention, and by directing it, there is an opposing mechanical force that pulls attention away. The only way I'm going to be able to climb the ladder of consciousness is through the division of attention to include two forces. As we are, in sleep, we are under the law of one, not under the law of three. That's identification. This struggle to call the attention to sensation is the beginning of real inner work. It's possible to experience a struggle with the attention by the friction between these two opposing forces until there's reconciliation. Gurdjieff called these the Holy Affirming, the Holy Denying, and the Holy Reconciling. Our problem is that in our sleep in life we have an "unholy denying." What should be our passive force, our personality, is under the illusion that it's active. It's not passive, as it should be, which is why I call it the unholy denying. We have to make it a Holy Denying force which would result in a passive/receptive personality.

We have to start by seeing the leaks and then learning to let them go. As we do exercises that bring us to presence, we start to awaken a bit; we start to see we are riddled with tensions. But if I try to relax, I can only relax so far. Here is where sensation is so important. The effort to *sense* brings me much further, brings a relaxation much deeper than if I just try to relax. The reason for this is I don't create sensation. Sensation is part of my essence. I was born with it. It exists as long as I am alive. Tensions and postures block out sensation. My experience is that relaxation is an important part of the way. However, using only relaxation will never bring the depth and quality of attention this work ultimately requires. As Bill Segal says in his book *Opening*, "I can be infinitely more relaxed than I am."

Self-remembering needs a finer energy that can be transformed from a pool of coarse energy. If you don't have enough coarse energy or lower energy, there won't be enough to be transformed. Gurdjieff tells us that nature supplies us with enough energy to work on ourselves and remember ourselves, at least for a period of time, but we often spend it all in negativity and dreams. Even our associations take a lot of energy. If I sit in a chair all day and just associate, I'm exhausted, more so than if I chopped down trees all day. If I'm aware of the energy of the mind, not the content, almost no energy is used! It even brings energy, because it can receive impressions. The same is true with feeling. If I am really feeling, I am enlivened, there is a joy of life. When I am in the body, even if I am exhausted, I could be filled with energy! If you find difficulty in sensing yourself or moving your sensation around the body, if you can't sense, you can use tension rather than relaxation and sensation. You can bring an exercise with a controlled tension. You very slightly tense your right arm, every muscle in that arm, very slightly, and what this will provide is the realization of the sensation of tension. Then you let go immediately; then you try sensing again. Then go to the right leg, tense the whole leg very slightly, and so on.

What does it mean to be aligned with gravity? With the distorted image we have of ourselves we're aligned with identification, using our energy going against gravity. Where is our real center of gravity? If the magnetism of the mind is the center of me, then I'm lopsided. The same is true with the feelings as well as the body. Very few people are aligned properly. When one looks at people one sees that everyone is leaning. There was a movie called *Little Big Man* in which Dustin Hoffman plays the role of a mixed race American Indian. There is a scene depicting a massacre, and Hoffman's character witnesses this slaughter of women and children. He later goes to the old Indian chief who is preparing to die and asks, "How could they possibly do this?" The Indian chief replied, "They don't know where the center of the Earth is." When I heard that, I was struck. I thought about this alignment, and how this represented being out of alignment. There is a center of gravity to everything, and being that we're not connected even to the center in ourselves, we're not connected to the center of the Earth, which could bring us to an organic alignment. This is why we see the horrors people cause on this

Earth. It is due to this lack of alignment! We are not children of Earth any more. We are children of the moon. We're not just under twenty-four or forty-eight laws. We're under many more unnecessary laws.

You need to relax. Relaxation and alignment are very important to learn and to practice. But remember, with tension and relaxation one can only go so far. With sensation you can go very far; you can even go past sensation of the flesh into a sensation of a new vibration. This may be what is called the Holy Ghost, or the chi energy. Throughout history it has been given many names. People experience it, but only in special states, or when they're more essential; it's imperceptible most of the time. There are times when it's there, yet because it's not a strong energy, an emotional energy, we don't realize what it is. Yet it will bring one real feelings and real mental energy. It is a physical energy that can bring you a new body, yet we don't know that body. What we know is sensation of the flesh. Some people in the Work make a God out of sensation. Sensation must be put in its correct place. If you overuse sensation, you're often just supporting your personality.

You have to expand your attention, start to open to the whole body; find hollowness where there are no obstacles to the movement of energy and attention. In this way one can sense the chi energy, or what I call in the Enneagram the "succeeding higher"; the vibration of the energy of hydrogen 24. One must experience and be acquainted with this subtle resonance, a circulation in every cell of the body. When one is trying to expand the mind into the body, first you have to have a body. As we are now, in sleep, one has only pieces of a body! That means being free of the content of the mind. When you work this way you can expand the energy of the mind into the body. One must spend many years in accelerated work to be able to do this. Eventually, one can expand with the feelings as well. This is like working on the structure of the vessel, like laminating the vessel with the energy of the mind, a coating with the texture of the emotions. Unless one has this basic vessel to hold these finer substances, one cannot accumulate anything. These forces are naturally striving to align us; allow them to take their rightful place. In fact, if we're present for long enough, we not only could have change of state, but

14

we could also have something deposited for change of being! We're learning how to use the law of Triamazikamno, the law of three. If we knew how to live under that law, we would be conscious very quickly. But we live under the law of one, maybe sometimes two.

"As I start to receive impressions, I start to see the unbecomingness of my life. Something awakens in me that I need very much. These moments are very important—in the reaction after that moment in which the space is filled anew I try to beautify the picture or change it, but not taking a new photograph. I must learn, again and again, to take another photograph. . ."

2

GROUP WORK

2.01   Q: Why is group work important?

JB: One of the principles I remember is that when you come to the Work, the one commitment you have to make is to come to the group meeting. Everything else is voluntary—Movements, work days or work periods, listening to music, whatever it is. It's all voluntary. The group is the foundation. Everything else springs from that. So let's try for six weeks or ten weeks and see what happens. But in reality, to be a member of the group, you commit to come to the group when you can. What we've seen is that people who are erratic in coming find it very difficult to work; they often stay the same, sometimes for years, or leave the Work.

The group work begins the process of enabling you to bring the Work into life. Because I believe in the beginning it's impossible to work in life. Nobody realizes the tremendous forces we are up against. We think that we are free. We don't realize we are in very strong currents.

One has the responsibility to understand the principles of the Work. You must make an effort to externally consider other group members. You don't gossip about the other people. At first you don't even socialize, because you're not there for that. Later you come to a point where it's good to socialize, because you need to become essence friends. Then there is a point where you need to go further than that, to bring external considering; in another way you work to help each other's consciousness. You become conscious friends, seekers of truth.

Group work establishes a procedure to bring an active force into your life, an *evolving* triad. It's not just one that discusses philosophy or even just Work ideas. There are special groups that just study the ideas. You do need to know the ideas. But group work is one way to go into life, with a task that's given. Later you may learn to give yourself a task. At the beginning, the group leader brings and represents a higher vibration, the vibration of consciousness or a level of consciousness. We struggle; we fail; personality is very active in us, but we are supported by the fact that we bring our experiences from these efforts back to the group, and the group leader's role is to bring to light to what idea this experience is related. We start to understand Gurdjieff's ideas not just from thinking and analyzing but from actually living the ideas. You may believe we're asleep, but that's not good enough; you must experience it. Very different, knowing we're asleep and experiencing the state of sleep. Usually, you experience it by waking up for a moment and realizing how deeply asleep you've been.

All of this work demands attention, bringing the attention out of the path of least resistance. As you bring in material from your struggle with tasks in life, your personal work starts to appear. What you see gives you the direction. Then if you work, the group leader could see a feature in you; but if you don't see, it doesn't do you any good. When you actually see a feature and bring in the experience of seeing more objectively, not one I seeing another I, but a larger seeing, then you could be given personal tasks in relation to that. Then you can use it as a reminding factor, as a way to maintain this higher vibration of consciousness in your life. This is what we need: we need to have our life be a reflection of an evolving triad. We don't have to worry about it at the beginning, at the involving part of it, or the Holy Denying; we have to bring the Holy Affirming, and with the help of the group, we find that we have an unholy denying, that we have an active personality that's completely erratic. These two active forces, active personality and the task, which also represents an active force, is the struggle I bring. I often get the opposite result for everything I want because personality is in total control and thinks that it's the center of the universe. The danger is I'll bring these personal tasks from the wrong energy or for personality profit or essence profit. Here is where I need the support of group work. With the help of the group leader a finer energy can be generated that can support this conscious struggle in life; and one sees that if one misses too many group meetings they can't struggle in life. They may want to but they can't. Another factor about a group is that it's a group of people that in general have little or nothing in common. They're not there for business or interested in money. They're not there for personality or because they like each other; they're not there for family, it's not blood. *They are there for consciousness.* That's the vibration that is like the string in a string of pearls, invisible. When you see a string of pearls you don't see the string, you see the pearls. A group is like that: maybe the right pearl necklace is worth a lot more than the individual pearls. In the Work, people often volunteer according to their nature. There are Work monks. They love the Work; they come because it's emotional for them; there are fakirs and yogis also. Then there are some people who are really Men No. 4. They commit to the Work, and they serve it not for personality or essence profit but because they're giving back what they received. They know it's for consciousness, real seekers of truth. Years ago I remember hearing that a group is like a stew. There are times some people bring the meat, some bring the carrots, some bring the peas, and some bring just a little broth because that's all they can bring. But a year later, the one who brought the broth now brings the meat; the one who brought the meat now brings the broth. From the point of view of the group leader, you have to see the group as a movable feast in a way. It's in motion; it's being cooked. People take different roles at different times, and as long as all the ingredients are there it's a dish, and it's a group. Every group is different, but it's hard to find people who are there for consciousness.

2.02   Q: Can you explain the inner work with interference, participation, and experimentation?

JB: That is almost unknown and was never written down. Orage learned it from Gurdjieff and brought it to certain people he worked with, like the Bensons and others. We know what interference is. What is participation? We need to develop a new center of gravity; for participation, you need a place to *be* that's free of the centers. You need to participate *with*, and it can't be one I participating with another I. Sensation does not participate *with*, sensation *separates* you, the separation of I from *it*.

Participation uses a new center of gravity. It's a place that's not from my ordinary centers. We find our work on interference is hard to give up. It takes a long time to shift the emphasis from interference towards participation. In participation, after I have established centering and this new center of gravity, I can follow myself much longer and see features that would never be able to be seen otherwise. However, we need a very strong attention that can be maintained for a longer time to participate adequately.

Experimentation is something very different. I put myself in situations. You could be with devils, as long as you're taking in impressions. Gurdjieff said, "No man friend—no man enemy, all are teachers." All are impressions. Experimentation comes in more at that level. You still have to go through interference and participation, but now you go through them quickly; they're not the emphasis of your work. Experimentation is a whole other kind of effort in which one opens to things that might not seem to make sense.

With interference, participation, and experimentation you have to know the order and how it works. You have to have someone who's traveled that road because there are many traps. Passive *Do* is a trap, even though without it you can't go anywhere; people can get trapped at passive *Do*, or at essence, or at Man No. 4—*all wonderful places*. But what is wonderful about Gurdjieff's Work is that it doesn't stop. Continued inner work would take you further. We have to develop receptivity to the energy of the higher centers.

2.03 Q: What is the purpose of the sitting in our Work? Can you expand on the history of the sitting? Can you explain different kinds of sittings done in private, quietly in a group, and guided sittings? At times you instruct us to follow the breath in a guided sitting. Can you explain the use of the breath in light of Gurdjieff's opinion against manipulating breathing?

JB: There are different versions of the history of the sitting. I've heard people say that Gurdjieff never gave sittings and that in their experience in the Work there were no sittings. All I know is that at the Foundation, when the sittings were first held, it was on a night that nobody else was there, and everyone who was brought to the sittings, especially at the beginning, was sworn to secrecy. We swore on our souls to Mme. de Salzmann that we would not talk about it, even to each other, so if you weren't at those sittings, you didn't know about them.

I was part of a group that was doing a history of the Work in America. We interviewed everybody we could find who knew Gurdjieff. One of the people we interviewed was Bill Segal. In that interview he said that he brought Mme. de Salzmann to Japan and afterwards he told her that with so many different Ways which have meditation practices coming to America, for the Work to survive and grow it needs a meditative process. And Bill Segal said that Mme. de Salzmann agreed, and from what he said, Mme. de Salzmann's words were, "What we should do is bring a way of meditating that Gurdjieff only worked on with his oldest people." Afterwards we had sittings in the Work. Not guided sittings; in fact, there was no such thing as a guided sitting as far as we knew. And later Mme. de Salzmann began what we now know as guided sittings. And as far as I know, I was one of the people who were there for the first guided sitting that she brought, again, sworn to secrecy. She said, "One day, maybe if you are given a role in which you lead people and help people, then you can speak. This will be up to you." This was something that was very unique to the Work, a guided sitting.

Later everybody was given what was called a collecting exercise. They weren't called sittings. They were short relaxation and sensation exercises. These exercises started out as active. There's receptivity in it as well, but one begins with an active force, taking the attention out of the path of least resistance. But there's a certain point where it changes, and your state then has to become receptive. It's according to what stage in the sitting you're referring to; it has *both* active and receptive.

From everything I know, there was no such thing as a guided sitting in *any* method, any tradition, until Gurdjieff brought it. Now there are people who use guided sittings, to some degree, in different paths. Our sitting is a much protected area. If it's done rightly, there's an active force which then becomes reconciled and then becomes receptive to a higher force. It's more of a living movement where one has to learn how to go from the ordinary state, which we start in, to a much higher state of vibration. *To be quiet and still is a very active movement.* If you're in the middle of a stream with a strong current, to be still will take a lot of effort.

There are different types of sittings: silent sittings, guided sitting in a group, and one's own personal sitting. The way we would begin is to have a collecting exercise in our own work, but when we come together we do a guided sitting. Eventually the material given in a guided sitting has to be incorporated into *my* own personal sitting.

The transformation of the energies we receive from following the breath comes from what Gurdjieff calls the "first conscious shock," remembering ourselves in front of an impression. It will cause the breath to go further in its transformation and transmutation of energies and bring me these higher energies and the coating for what he calls a "higher being body," or astral body. *In this Work we don't interfere with the breath.* Somebody told me they were doing some exercise, in which they breathe in one nostril and breathe out the other or take short, quick breaths; all these are manipulations of the breathing. Right now the breath is basically controlled by the instinctive center. The last thing we want is the breath to be controlled by the wrong center; people do damage to themselves that way. I see that when I'm in my head, I hold my breath, and then I gasp, and then I hold my breath again. In general, that's the way I breathe, not very deeply. I don't let the out-breath go; I don't breathe out very far. Mme. de Salzmann once described it "as if we're afraid to breathe out." If I'm in my emotions, I find my breathing is a short and rapid, and it's only when I'm present in my body that I find that I breathe from the abdomen. The state I'm in and where I am determines the way I breathe. Even if I try to change my breath, my *present* state will bring the breath right back. Often we try to use the mind to control the breath. If you follow Gurdjieff's indications, you don't try to manipulate the breath. I bring my attention *to* the breath, I let the breath guide my attention, and I *follow* the breath. The breath will find its way deeper inside me and will find its way to places that the attention needs to go. I can't bring it there. I need to trust the breath; when I follow the breath, it normalizes. My state changes, I'm not in my head or my feelings, in my postures and tensions, and I can start to be more centered. The breath will find its origin. In my own personal experience, I found blockages in my diaphragm, tensions that felt like steel. It took a long time to erode the tensions, but even when I did the diaphragm would vibrate violently. When I finally got rid of the tensions, it was such a blessing for me, and I hadn't even realized I had them until I started to lose them.

Mme. de Salzmann told us there are three kinds of breath; the ordinary breath, which comes from whichever center is dominating; a breath that comes from the abdomen; and a third breath that comes from the initiating energy of life, which *I* consider the vibration of hydrogen 24, the real energy of the body. The breath could come from there. It's as though I'm breathing with every cell because that resonance is from the whole body. Every energy has its own circulation. Gurdjieff tells us we have nodules or nerve centers around the body, but because we have a little clump of them in our solar plexus, that's where we usually *experience* emotions. These are doorways into the centers. The circulations have to expand throughout the whole of each center and the whole body. The breath is a substance; the lungs keep some of it; some of it is breathed out; but if one is conscious, or aware of oneself, remembering oneself, there's something extra from the breath that stays or settles in the body. It's not the breath; it's the vibration, the energy. It's a visualization that helps you come to this resonance in the body. You're not creating it; you're opening to it. The breath is very useful in that way as well. But manipulation of the breath will only create damage and takes it away from the instinctive center, which one really doesn't want to do.

Someone once told me, "I stopped doing the sitting in the morning. It was so difficult, so I do it at night and get much more than I did when I did it in the morning."

In the Work there are times when you do sittings at night as well as in the morning. At night you can go much deeper because you're out of the current of life. There is no opposition: the body is already a little tired; you're ready to go to bed; and you don't struggle as hard against this force that sweeps us through our lives. The sitting in the morning is an active force; the sitting at night is a passive/receptive force.

The minute you wake up, you're in the current of life. It's still a little diminished because it's morning; personality hasn't been totally activated yet, you still have a chance. When you try, later, to bring your attention against a current of life that has many calls, many pulls, you have almost no chance. You're exercising an attention in your sitting. It's like weights in a gym. You don't just pick up a weight or just put it down. You use that weight in order to strengthen certain muscles; there are different exercises to strengthen different muscles. It's very hard to do the sitting in life, though it is possible. The current is much stronger, which is why we do the collecting exercise as preparation. If we didn't do the collecting exercise in the morning, we'd have almost no chance in life. We have nothing but leaks in us, so we've already wasted energy. We need to collect ourselves and accumulate a certain vibration of a higher order that could be the active force in life; otherwise we have nothing that could take that role. The collecting exercise opens up the possibility of struggle. It deposits something in us—energy—because to struggle you need energy and later one needs to bring the essence of the sitting into life, for instance, self-remembering in front of an impression.

The guided meditation we do in groups is both active *and* passive. According to which stage we're at, it's really the first and second triad of the Enneagram. The first triad is interference, and the second triad is participation. It's the same thing with the sitting. The first part is interference, the collecting against the pulls of each center, of life: you're collecting your attention; you're collecting your centers; you're collecting everything. Once you've opened to a finer energy, it brings you to the second triad, participation. When you have this resonance, you can then open to the question, "How can I receive an impression?" I have to be aware and be present. As I said, there are the three *P*'s: patience, persistence, and presence—the three *P*'s in a pod, so to speak.

2.04 Q: We talk a lot about the guided meditation. I was just wondering about the quiet meditation that we sometimes take.

JB: I know certain older people who only bring silent sittings. There's a danger in the Work, which is that you can become too humble! And, you know, there are two sides to that stick: one is total arrogance and power possessing, and the other side of it is this humility of, "Oh, we really can't know anything." Somebody who has been in the Work her whole life, she knew Gurdjieff, once said at a meeting, "We don't know anything, and when we take a group they know as much as us." My response is, if we really don't know anything after forty years in the Work, why don't we lock the doors of the Foundation and leave because certainly we're not getting anything. I don't agree with that. I think most older people in the Work know a hell of a lot more than younger people in the Work, we've had a lot more experiences, and hopefully we've changed innerly.

My groups once went to Sparkhill for a work day. They usually didn't give sittings there, but we sort of insisted. Lady Pentland was going to give the sitting, and I was concerned that she might have planned a silent sitting. So I said, "Lady Pentland, I would like to ask you to really give a sitting. I know you were there, in the same group as me, when Mme. de Salzmann gave guided sittings, year after year after year." She said, "We'll see." And then she gave a marvelous sitting, really wonderful, because she *had* been there.

In my groups, I took it upon myself to bring the guided sittings as purely as possible, the way Mme. de Salzmann originally gave them, and there are others that did that too, like Paul Reynard and Frank Sinclair and Pierce Wheeler, a number of people who really tried to bring the sittings as purely and accurately as possible, to transmit them.

I don't just imitate her sitting in the moment. I try to *live* it. It is possible to share your state, and here the demand is to express it

25

in words. You're describing something that is living now, it's not memory or from your head. I don't agree that all the people who had been in Mme.'s sittings should necessarily give sittings themselves. There are some who are better at giving sittings than others; for example, I've been with people you have to block out when you sit because they're speaking entirely from their heads. A sitting should not be guided if it can't be guided in the right way.

It's up to people in the Work who know to train people to bring guided sittings. I train my older people to give sittings. It's through giving the sittings that they learn how. They've experienced enough sittings so that they have the material, but it takes a while to be able to be free enough of personality to give one correctly. To give a sitting is quite an event. One has to be in the moment. *Everything* has to get out of the way and be at the service of the moment. There's a transmission and there needs to be a pathway. And this is what most people don't understand, that there actually is a pathway in the sitting.

2.05 Q: From the perspective of the Work, what could be meant by prayer? What is the difference between prayer and meditation?

JB: When you use prayer as a petition, you are asking to change the order of the universe because everything is in a certain order. The preposterous ego or ignorance involved in thinking that you could reach God directly is extraordinary. I once asked Mme. de Hartmann if there was a prayer for people in the Work. She said, "Yes, I asked Mr. Gurdjieff the same question and his answer was, 'Thank you, Lord, for giving me one more day to work on myself.'" When one thinks of what's at stake, the reality of accumulating astral matter, finer vibrations, and learning to know myself through self-observation, every day is valuable. What I see is that I waste every day. I do a certain amount of work, but I don't really feel the extraordinariness of having one more day. The idea of thanking the Lord is different from asking for something. You are not petitioning to be given something; this is a different kind of prayer; it's recognition of what's at stake.

Edgar Cayce was asked about the difference between prayer

26

and meditation, and he answered, "Prayer is asking the Lord for something, while meditation is listening for the answer." I thought it was a wonderful explanation. Meditation is a receptive force; prayer is an active force. In the Work meditation plays a different role. We call it a sitting, but it is very different than what most of the world calls meditation. If we have the *right meditation*, one that is receptive, bringing the attention to sensation is what I call, bringing attention out of the path of least resistance. First you have to collect your attention. This is why many times we begin with what we call a collecting exercise. I was told that when Mme. de Salzmann was asked about the sensation of the whole body, she said, "First you need an order because if you go immediately to the whole body, it's very vague and one could lose oneself very quickly in dreams. But with an order you cannot lose yourself so easily."

Many times what people call meditation peace is often actually an attracted attention. I am pulled into another part of the body or my feelings. The struggle is to collect the attention or the energy of each center. Regardless of your state when you struggle with your morning collecting exercise you are bringing order, which means the attention can't go wherever it wishes; this is the struggle. In meditation we are trying to work with the energies of all the centers; it's possible to be open to all the centers at once.

The centers are alien to each other. They don't even speak the same language. They are not at the same tempo. They don't have the same associations or the same I's. *But they need to know each other.* In meditation or in a sitting, I can start to bring the centers into a relationship so they coexist for a moment. This is a great demand because it means the attention has to open and be divided to include two forces. The attention has to be divided as equally as possible, 50/10. In the beginning it's usually more like 90/10. This is a work for a lifetime. We're after something more valuable than diamonds. We are asking for and trying to *buy* what is perhaps the most expensive material in the world. We think we can buy it with our counterfeit or Monopoly money. One can't expect consciousness or an astral body in a week or a month.

One must find a new center of gravity within oneself that can exist, expand, and stay within the whole. Then the whole has a center of gravity it revolves around, and it has its own atmosphere. With the magnetizing of the centers there is no atmosphere, but with a center of gravity there is a materiality that develops drop by drop. It's here that one begins a new level of work, where the centers are no longer alien to each other. In this new center of gravity there's a new vibration, the source of a circulation that exists in every cell of the body.

The energy of the mind must expand into the whole body and by dividing my attention the formatory associations weaken. As these associations weaken, I will see that there is a *special something* behind the associations; and that special something needs to come into my body and start to coexist in a whole new way.

Mme. de Salzmann once said, very beautifully, "I cannot do it, but without me it will not be done." I cannot do this, but laws exist that will do the work for me, such as the law of three and the law of triadic attraction. The law of three does not consist of three *isolated* forces; there is an attraction between the forces, like gravity. If I can maintain this equal attention simultaneously on the energy and the resonance of the mind and body, then the law of triadic attraction, which I believe is what Mme. de Salzmann calls "self-tuning," comes into play, and these two energies which normally repel each other will start to be drawn towards each other. We need to allow the emotions to become the third force. It has a different "color" than the energies of the mind and body. Where is the emotional energy to come from? As I am, it is not available to me. I don't know what it is to have faith, love, and hope, or even vibrations that would produce that. I have coarse vibrations that produce self-pity, self-love, and negative reactions of all kinds. To experience what I just described in a few minutes takes many years of practicing again and again, day after day after day, and losing myself again and again. That's a very big initiation when you start to work from there. Meditation in the Work is what I have just described. If there is no inner movement that starts to bring the centers into a relationship, it's not real meditation.

2.06 Q: I originally asked about prayers because I know you

28

use prayer in your sitting, and it is different from any other prayer I know. Can you talk about the prayer I Wish to Be Myself?

JB: One of the techniques of Gurdjieff that I found through Mme. de Hartmann is the prayer I Wish to Be Myself, or the variation, I Wish to Remember Myself. The canon which supports this prayer I Wish to Be Myself brings the attention to I in the head; "wish" in the solar plexus; "to be" in the spine; and "myself" in the whole lower part, including the abdomen, sexual area, and legs, what the Taoists call the "sea of elixir." So, when you say "I" you sense the energy of the mind; when you say "wish" you sense the energy of the emotions; when you say "to be" you sense your spine; when you say "myself" you sense the whole lower part. This is more a practice than a prayer. You are creating a relationship among the centers. Used in the right way, there are not only the words but an inner movement. If you just keep repeating the same words again and again it becomes mechanical.

This practice has many sides to it. There is a spot between the eyes where Indians from India put a red mark, the bindhi; in Judaism, portions from the Torah are put in a small box of the tefillin in the same spot between the eyebrows or just above that. I found that spot to be like a doorway into the mind that can be used to quiet the associative mind. It's not a doorway into the energy of the higher mental center, but into the energy of the head itself.

With "wish" you have a doorway to the feelings behind the breastbone. Usually I block what is behind the breastbone from my awareness. I don't want to experience the chaos that is behind the breastbone.

For "to be" we have the spine, the doorway into the whole body.

For "myself" there's a place where something could be born. I bring not only the three centers, I also bring the sexual and instinctive centers—a place where there may be a void, an empty place that I was given where something, a new center of gravity, could be born.

This is a practice that needs to be done at the beginning, during, or after every sitting. It could also be done at any time, depending on the circumstances, and even open to a higher question.

For instance, now you have the energy of the head, but what is I? I don't sense I, I sense a lower energy that has stolen the sense of I. Similarly, what is "wish"? The energy of "wish" that I have now is not very high. "To be": How much being do I really have? "Myself": Who am I? How can I bring this ultimate question to work in life?

2.07 Q: I sometimes ask, "Who am I?" or "What am I?" What part do these questions play in my work?

JB: These are what could be called sacred questions. What makes them sacred is that they're not just questions for the mind; they're inquiries and a search, it's a search for the unknown: "What am I?" or "Who am I?" Even though they seem similar, they're different questions and they can be used for different reasons. And I find they evoke different responses in different individuals.

One could use a question as a way to interfere with ordinary personality. I ask, "Who am I?" and I search, and it's like demanding a more conscious attention, a presence, sensation, to maintain the question for at least a short while, and one may see one's personality. It could be used in that way. When you're trying to remember yourself in front of an impression, asking "Who am I?" becomes very important. If one could have this sense of I am-ness for a moment, this impression of that moment, a much finer energy is generated by the transformation of substances from air, physical food, and impressions.

Mme. de Salzmann brought this question to my group, but I wasn't ready for it at the time; it didn't burn. When I asked, "Who am I?" it only reverberated in my mind. The biggest problem we have with this question is that the mind steals it. There was a great sage in India at the first half of the twentieth century, Bhagavan Ramana Maharshi, who would only work with this question, "Who am I?" He said that this question is not for the mind. At one point he gave an example: to have the mind ask this question is like dressing the thief up as a policeman in order to catch the thief.

One summer, I must have been in the Work maybe eight or nine years, Mme. de Hartmann gave me a book by Bhagavan Ramana Maharshi called *Day by Day with Bhagavan*, and there's a section called "Self-inquiry," which is based on how to bring this question, and it further acquainted me with this question "Who am I?" As usual, during that summer the Foundation closed. Almost all Work with groups would stop, and usually I would go into a deep state of identification year after year. Then when the Foundation finally opened again I would say "Thank God." That summer I read *Day by Day with Bhagavan* and something changed; and I started to burn, like when you rub twigs together. I started to bring the question wherever I went. I remember dancing at a disco with a beautiful girl, and what I was saying inside myself was, "Who am I?" And then I started to use the techniques and the tools of the Work, *not to wake up, but to not fall asleep*, because I knew I would lose this question. Even at sittings, I'd be doing the sitting that I was given and at the same time I'd be searching for "Who am I?" I remember vividly one sitting, where I saw a whole sheaf of tensions and a picture of myself tied to an emotional state. I saw that as being the lie of I, and I suddenly relaxed, going much deeper in myself. I saw everything that said I in me was a lie. In fact, I felt as though I was walking through the Land of Not I, that was my formulation; but there were certain moments where I felt there was an opening to feeling, something of what life *could* be, and that what Gurdjieff calls "permanent I" was not a big or small I but it was something very different, *unique*! I started to have a much deeper feeling and a new kind of sincerity. Something was starting to drastically change from this burning question that I was able to maintain.

One weekend that summer I had a chance to talk to Mrs. Sutta, my group leader at the time, and I thought, "Now I have a chance to get her advice and opinion," and so I mentioned what was going on with me. She said, "No, no, it's imagination. You couldn't have this." When she said that something in me crumbled, I couldn't make the effort any more, and that's where that burning ended, as though she threw water on the fire and it went out. I remember that vividly. I have no idea what would have happened, maybe it would have gone anyway, and I can't say that I would have been able to maintain that. I had such trust in her; something deep in me had trusted her to such a degree; but later I realized it was because she didn't even know what I was talking about, *she hadn't had this experience.* All this showed me how valuable that question was.

I have found that the question "What am I?" can evoke the *sensation* of I more easily, and the question "Who am I?" evokes the *feeling* of I more directly. We worked for a long time with Mme. de Salzmann on the *sensation* of I, not I *have* a sensation, but the *sensation* of I-am-ness, and some time later we worked on the *feeling* of I-am-ness. Then there are the questions "Where is the center of myself? Where is my source?" Even in the first triad of the Enneagram, and in our work with interference, when I am given a task to sense my left leg in front of someone or at a certain time, this actually represents the physical aspect of the question "Who am I?" Because in order for me to bring a free attention, a conscious attention to sense that left leg, there's a demand that I awaken and search for I. The effort itself, without the words, is a demand for the feeling of I. This is why I call tasks surgical instruments: they're much more important than we could possibly imagine because they all are a demand for I, if they are approached with a right kind of effort. They have to demand a free attention and they need to be done for consciousness, not for personality or essence profit. If these requirements are met, the tasks are different forms of the one question "Who am I?" Even in the work on interference using the representatives of self-remembering, impressions that we get of ourselves, of active personality, are impressions which bring us new material. That prepares us for real self-remembering in front of an impression. This effort is what brings us first to conscious shock and later to work on participation, which is the road to transform us further and further until even the energy of H6 can exist in us. This is our aim. The name of God is I Am That I Am.

What could be permanent I has to be three-centered; it has to be the energies of the mind, feeling, and body, together. We need to create a new, special place in us that the mind and the body and the emotions can't get to, the void. Everyone has to develop an opening to that place; I can exist from there, a higher I can be deposited there. That can begin with I that starts in the head with the word, but it's really the I of the whole of oneself, and being centered in a lower place in oneself, or in the solar plexus. One could have a real visualization, like I in the head; conceptual I, "wish" in the solar plexus; and "I can," again the conceptual I, or a sense of I of the whole body, and "can" in the spine, or "I am."

You must get a sense of different centers, the mind, the body, and the feelings; so these kinds of exercises—"I wish," "I can," "I am"—vivify the centers and invigorate the search for I. We can't search for it in our fantasies. We have to bring this search for I with a higher presence. It seemed to me that I could open to this search from any cell in the body. I couldn't allow any cell in the body to go unobserved. I had to be totally connected with everything; such vigilance brought these kinds of experiences. I had seen this in my search for "Who am I?" I remember feeling, "I cannot get disconnected from any part." I was able to understand the importance of the way the contents of the centers are glued or attached to each other by the law of accident. I had a picture, a concept of myself; I had a whole structure of postures, and I had a feeling; they were like a garment and they fell off. The postures and tensions that supported it, worry and anxiety that would be there when I saw that connection; the sheaf would fall away.

I've brought the work I just described to groups over the years, sometimes as the work on interference, sometimes as work on participation, even as experimentation. But when I bring this as participation, with groups that are ready for it, it has to be repeated many times, and then see who connects, who can keep these efforts as a pure inquiry of attention without the mind stealing it. The mind will always try. But suddenly, one person out of the group takes this on in the right way and tries to struggle. On some people it's had a remarkable effect, leading to other work, helping them a lot.

There were times when I would say to the group, "You're really not working on this the way I have brought it." And they would say, "What do you mean? Of course we are." I'd say, "No." They'd say, "How do you know?" And the reason I knew is because they were not bringing in the right results.

2.08 Q: People come to work events to get their "Work

injection." Can you explain this potential danger and how to avoid it?

JB: When I first came to the Work we were warned not to come for this, what we called a Work injection. The Work is for change of being. It's not to feel better or get relief. For example, I would come to a group sometimes so tense that just to be relieved of those tensions was like manna from heaven. It was like great food. I loved it. I would walk out of the group and feel this is incredible, this state I am in. I got my work injection! But that's change of state, and it's very important to differentiate between change of state and change of being, or transformation of state and transformation of being. Change of state is of the moment, a day, or a week. Change of being is a year, a decade, a lifetime. This Work is a work for change of being.

There are many spiritual ways that are better than the *Work* for a change of state. Visit a holy guru and sit by his side, get the benefits of his presence and feel a very high energy. But the minute you walk out the door you put back on your postures, your tensions, your anxieties, your values; you go back to the center of gravity of your level of being.

But you do need these higher vibrations in order to be able to go into life and see yourself, to begin to know thyself! Why? I start to develop an attention that could be divided between I and it. This is the aim, the core of this Work. A group of people trying to be present generates energy; there are Movements which give you a lot of energy; there are readings and discussion groups. It actually works very well, you get your Work injection, but there is one big problem: personality can hide in that glow of vibration; your features can hide; your buffers can hide. It isn't that you get to certain energy and hope that your personality will appear; you have to bring that struggle with this energy into the moment to see your personality. This energy was given to you to help you struggle throughout the week. It's only in life that these features will be exposed. And without a carrier, how do you do it? You need to develop a vessel that can hold this holy water of vibrations. Everything in life causes you to spill it.

There is a story of a man who came to a conscious man and said, "I wish to be conscious." This teacher lived in a beautiful

34

mansion with many flowers and paintings on the walls, and he said, "I can help you." The teacher filled a spoon with olive oil and said, "Take this spoon of oil and carry it through every room in the house without spilling it." The man tried and soon spilled the oil. He tried again and again and finally was able to carry the spoon of oil through the house without spilling it. Then the teacher said, "Now take the spoon and walk through the house, but when you come back I want you to describe every painting," which meant he couldn't look at the spoon. Let's say that once he acquired that ability, he was conscious. To carry the spoon without spilling it, without looking at it, taking in impressions: Doesn't that represent remembering yourself in front of impressions? It's the Work as we know it. So without a spoon how are we going to do that? Without the spoon or the vessel, you can't even attempt this work of change of being.

2.09 Q: What is the meaning of the designations first, second, and third lines of Work? What is the importance of each of these lines, and how are they related to each other?

JB: Even the Work itself must follow the law of Heptaparaparshinokh, the law of seven; and Triamazikamno, the law of three. Everyone begins with one commitment, first line of Work, attendance at the group meetings, and personal struggles.

The basic principles of the Work are:
-respect for one's group leader;
-respect for the other people in the group, to externally
  consider them and not slander them,
-to feel gratitude that one is receiving something higher;
-to be sincere with one's group and group leader;
-not to speak about what is said in group meetings to
  anyone outside.

One of the things we discover when we are in a group is that we come to intervals. Suddenly, the work becomes dry, and we feel a need for something to go further. At first, intervals are small. Maybe an activity such as Movements can bring a shock to get you past that interval. Gurdjieff tells us that the first shock comes from outside. The second shock needs to come from inside to complete the octave. This is the basic law and it applies to the Work as well.

Second line of Work is the work against self-will. For seven years, when Mme. Ouspensky was alive, I went to Mendham for work days, sometimes weekends or even weeks at a time. There were many times during these work periods when a job would be given, and you could see that you approached it with an attitude of how *I* think it should be done, bringing in *my* personality and requirements. One principle was that *you were expected to take on the job as given.* Some people, including me, just *couldn't* and had to argue, and one would see and suffer one's personality. Even though I remembered this principle of the Work, I always tried my own version and it was obvious to the group leaders, who would say, "Mr. Brewster, just do your job as given." Another principle was that if you were blamed for something, you would accept the blame, even if you weren't at fault! One had to understand that even if you didn't do it *this* time, you probably did the same thing a thousand times before and didn't get caught. I struggled to keep from saying, "Wait a minute, I didn't do that." Years later, when I found myself being unfairly blamed in life, I found it almost impossible *not* to accept blame. It was always a struggle, but I remembered the principle, and it woke me up. Second line of Work is filled with principles like that. This is a practice of going against self-will.

The important thing is to create this bridge between inner work you do in groups and life. One of the most difficult, almost impossible things you can do is to bring the Work into the powerful currents of life. One of the methods is working in life with a task, with support of others in the group who are trying the same task at the same time. There were times at Mendham when we were not given tasks in the morning, so one had to bring one's own task, one's own work. One needs to struggle to come to second line of Work with a question. If you don't have a question, it is always important to remember to bring work from your group or a personal task previously given.

Work periods can be used as a shock bridge to see oneself. The work periods made visible the things about ourselves that are invisible in life. This is due to the interaction with people. Working

36

with others helps you maintain a work with the support and energy of others while in action.

There is a point when one reaches a certain level or an interval where third line of Work is required, the principle being *work for the Work*. The third line of Work is a way which serves the needs and aims of the Work itself on a large scale, not just for my own benefit or the benefit of a small group, but for the benefit of furthering the aims of the Work. You have to sacrifice your own requirements and needs to serve the Work in a larger sense. There are many ways to serve the Work and what the Work needs. Third line of Work is for people able to do third line of Work.

2.10 Q: Gurdjieff said that all personal relationships one has with other people are *merde* and that you must free yourself from personal relationships with other people, except with your family, from which you can't and you shouldn't try. What does that mean?

JB: You got that from the 1940s meetings? You must totally disregard that. He was speaking to an individual. Never try an exercise or take what he says as the absolute truth for *everyone*! Maybe that person needed to hear that. We read it, and we think it applies to everybody; but maybe he would tell somebody else the complete opposite. You've got to be careful about reading transcripts of group meetings Gurdjieff hosted. For one thing, they are translations, and you should not take that in a general way. That's why some people say there's a lot of contradiction in these transcripts.

2.11 Q: Can you say something about the difference in the development between men and women?

JB: Mme. de Hartmann once said, jokingly, "You know, it's really easier for women because they are already in their emotions, so they just have to develop their mind. Men are in their mind, so they have to go to their feelings, develop their feelings, and then they've got to go back to their mind. So it takes them a little longer." We laughed about it, but in a way there's a truth there. And Gurdjieff speaks about that difference too, he says that, "In women emotions are a little more developed and men's minds are a little more developed."

When I came to the Work, it was separated; there was men's

37

work and women's work. But that was physical. Mme. de Salzmann brought us the sittings; women sat on one side, men on the other side. Certainly there's a difference between men and women in personality and in essence. I think in active *Re* H48, which is methods of the Work, there could be a difference in the sense that women may need a little more work on the mind at times and men may need a little bit more work on the emotions.

It's not the development of the center. The number one thing is where you make your decisions from: With which centers are you most identified? Which center does your I-in-quotation-marks come from? There's a woman I know, a group leader, an excellent mind, but she's always been stuck in her emotions. She has never gotten past that. I remember once the two of us had a meeting with Mme. de Salzmann, and at one point Madame said to me, "I see that the energy passes in you." And this woman said, "In me?" Madame said, "No, no, with you," and she pointed right to the woman's solar plexus, "everything stops here." And I felt it was true. And this woman told me she cried for two days after that, which proves the point! And I thought about it for two days. Unfortunately, in my estimation, she still has that barrier. Now, my barrier may be that I don't feel enough, so I can't put myself above her or anyone. For me, the mind has become much stronger.

When you get past that, when you get to the energy of H24 it's free of gender, no more male or female. When there is a vibration of H24 in a room, and there are men and women there, it's all the same. In the Gnostic Gospel according to St. Thomas, it seemed that Mary Magdalene was sitting with Jesus and his disciples, and they said, "Why do you allow Mary to be with us? She's a woman." And Jesus responded, "Let us say I will make her male." And I feel that he was speaking about this energy that exists and is beyond gender.

2.12 Q: It has been said that in order to progress to the next rung on the ladder, one must first put someone on his own rung.

JB: There is a process and a succession in the way the Work is brought. My teachers understood they were serving very high forces, and that in order to move up you had to put someone on your rung. I am sure not all of them liked me or loved me because of my personality or my dimpled smile, or the fact that I would do anything for them. I think some of them saw a possibility that I might be able to fit on a higher rung someday, and *that* was important to them because they understood this law. They gave of themselves and provided you with the work you needed to go further. This law is extraordinary; when applied objectively, it is the mechanism that cleanses the Work, keeps it pure, in a line of development, and avoids the corruption that afflicts many Ways. What stops this line of development is corruption of the kind that comes through nepotism or likes and dislikes of people. I was thinking recently, why is it that the children of leaders become the next leaders? The leader had to create the position, but to the child it is given, a very different process, yet it takes place. At a time when we need more conscious leadership we get less conscious leadership. What they don't realize is that they are breaking a sacred law. And this stops everyone from going further and is the cause of a deviation in the correct direction within that group. People don't realize what's at stake. One has to think what it means to put someone on your rung of the ladder: that means you start to evaluate people, not by whether you like them or whether they are good for your ego or whether they help you or even whether they are good for the group, but to judge them by their growth and their potential level of being—ultimately, by whether they have the potential to actually take your rung.

At the bottom rungs, there is no problem; there are enough people to take these rungs. But as you move up the ladder, there are not as many people, and fewer and fewer as you go further. At some point there may be only one person who can take your rung, and that may be the one person you just can't stand, but if you really see this, you understand that he or she has the potential to leave that rung and take yours; that process purifies the work. I'm on a rung right now which I have worked to achieve for many years. I'm on a certain level; this is why I am working with my assistants and the younger group leaders that are developing. Why do I give so much time, even to brand new people? It is because I don't know who will be able to climb the ladder. Everyone has a tempo as they climb the ladder. Not everybody goes at the same pace. The person on the higher rung has to have a vision that takes in everybody. It is very important that there be this vision.

I once went to the president of the Foundation to inform him that I was starting a new group in Connecticut. I was asked why this was necessary. Why focus so much on beginners? Imagine if that had been said to Mme. de Hartmann when she was about to introduce the de Salzmanns to Gurdjieff! Without Mme. de Salzmann, our Work would not be the same! There is a succession in the way the Work is brought. My teachers were giants because they understood they were serving very high forces.

There will always be an opposing force. The Work is never convenient to life; life is never convenient to the Work. Otherwise, maybe life forces will win or overcome the Work forces. But there are angels working for the Work, not just devils working against it. There are also conscious forces working against the Work. The ray of creation is an involutionary octave. The idea that Satan was part of God, this is the idea of the Hasnamuss; as is the destructions of the holy labors of Ashiata Shiemash from within by power-possessing beings. I have never heard anyone speak about that, but I saw it take place. Gurdjieff said we didn't have to worry about it *then*, but maybe we do *now*. In Gurdjieff's time there was nothing to worry about, but later there were some people who used the Work to go against the Work, to destroy the real inner Work. When I recognized this I thought, "My God, how did Gurdjieff know about this?"

I don't think I ever heard anyone, in the entire fifty-three years I have been in the Foundation, speak about this law. I brought it out a couple of times and everybody pushed it aside, yet it is a key principle in the Work. Why do I put someone on my rung? *It's the way the Work works!* That's why I am investing my time with certain people, some whom I like and some whom I don't like on a personal level, but they are all valuable, they're extraordinary, heroes; they are all struggling, even some who seem to be failing. You never know who will be the next Mme. de Salzmann.

2.13 Q: We know there are some groups today that no longer have a group leader. What are your thoughts about this kind of situation?

40

JB: My first thought is that it goes against what I understand Gurdjieff brought us. There are certain types of work in which people can come together and work without a leader, such as readings and group projects. But I believe there is a necessary hierarchy for a group involving a ladder of vibrations. One is always active in relation to a lower triadic vibration, and one must become receptive to a higher triadic vibration which is brought by the group leader or an objective vision.

When a group leader dies or it happens that a group came together artificially, maybe they say, "We don't want a new group leader. We now can work on our own and generate a vibration." But I believe it goes against the principles that Gurdjieff brought about how the group work works.

What do we need a group leader for? The biggest obstacle to unity is chief feature. Chief feature is the foundation of the entire mechanical structure of personality; it is what stands in the way of having a center of gravity within oneself, unification, and yet it's invisible. It's the last thing we would even admit to having. Without someone who understands the way to see chief feature, it's almost impossible to see. However, there is a way; there are methods, exercises, and pathways which will bring you in front of your chief feature. This work is usually forgotten. The groups that I know about in the Foundation that are leaderless really need someone who can help them work on chief feature because they have not seen it yet.

There also may be groups where the group leader doesn't live there, who works through email, telephone, occasional visits, but there is still a group leader. But a group alone, where is the triad? Where is the higher force coming from? That is the question.

We know that when the teacher comes, everybody comes together; but when the teacher is not there, they all are apart. Is it possible for a group to function, to be receptive, if some of the people in the group are not on that level, don't have the same level of understanding or experiences?

There could be a group of Men No. 4, of group leaders that have a group leader but not in a physical form. They've taken on working together to actualize the aims of Gurdjieff; the aims of

41

vibrations H12 and H6, the higher centers, an objective vision of what Gurdjieff intended for the Work in the world, serving a higher purpose. Does the Work have a purpose in this world? I believe it does. Maybe we can't know it. Gurdjieff said, "The Fourth Way comes into the world for a reason, it appears, and then when its reason is over it disappears again." I believe the reason for the Fourth Way isn't here yet because it takes generations for it to develop to the right level. Mme. de Salzmann said, "Unless the Work produces a certain level of vibrations in the world terrible things will happen." Are we producing that vibration? What is the evidence? Maybe we need to wait and be patient and hope, but a group on the level of Man No. 4, or higher, whose lives are devoted to the Work and vibrate at a certain vibration could be receptive to H12 or higher, representing a real teacher.

One day it was discovered that there existed
a monastery that had been out of touch
with the main body of the Church for as far
back as anyone could remember.
The church decided to send an emissary to
the island to make sure that the monks were still
adhering to the correct forms and prayers.
He found the monks sincere and especially
devout but that in many places their prayers
were in the wrong order.
After showing them their errors and
instructing them in the correct practices,
he felt very satisfied that
he had put them on the right path.
The next day, after leaving on the boat, he
was standing by the rail thinking what a good
job he had done when he suddenly heard a shout.
Looking up, he couldn't believe his eyes.
There was one of the monks running on top
of the water towards the boat. When the monk
caught up he found the priest and asked, "Sir, we
were confused about one item; did you say to do
the morning prayers at 6:00 AM or at 7:00?"

*"Personality has a way of turning you from work,
making you feel uncomfortable, without a role.
It's personality's way of trying to divert you
from a much larger Work.
Suffer the discomfort,
stay with it; wait; the discomfort will soon be gone,
comfortable in the emptiness, not having
a role to play."*

3

PERSONALITY

3.01 Q: If there is a difference between ego and personality, what is it?

JB: Most of the time ego is invisible. I don't see it; in fact, *I am the ego*. I define that as active personality. Ego runs the world. People die unnecessarily because of it. Everything's a triad, so there's always a part that's lower. There's ego on every level; every frequency of vibration has its own relationship to ego. The aim of that ego is to satisfy an illusion or the lie about myself: that's active personality, everything is about me, me, me; I want, my requirements, and it's all for personality's profit. The idea of personality profit and even essence profit is very useful to help me identify it. Without knowing this idea, I'll never see my ego, unless somebody says something to me that doesn't meet my requirements and I'm present enough to receive that impression.

Then there's the ego of the essence, an I-am-ness. It does have an ego, but it's a much better, healthier ego than personality's.

There's ego, and then there's another kind of ego about which Gurdjieff said, "One must become a conscious egoist before one could become an altruist."

And then there's the ego of Man No. 4, which is the ego of consciousness. I need this ego to evolve. There's ego, but I act from a truth about myself, not the usual lie of personality. The ego of Man

No. 4 is really what Gurdjieff means when he speaks about a more conscious egoist.

3.02 Q: What is the effect of ego on our centers?

JB: We need to consider that our centers are contaminated and ego is one of the forces behind a lot of the contamination. There is a something put into all sentient beings that comes from a very high place, *the real need to be.* Since I don't yet have being, that need gets twisted into ego. I create a fantasy with the contents of my centers, an illusion of being. I remember a story to illustrate this point. One day the Devil is stoking the furnaces in Hell, and one little imp comes running to him and says, "Oh my God, Satan, we have a great problem. We're going to have to shut down Hell." The Devil screams, "What are you talking about? We're going to shut down Hell? I know we're only half full because people don't have a soul so we don't get too much material down here. You know, you have to have a soul in order to get into Hell." So he said, "What do you mean, we're going to have to shut down?"

The imp says, "I just found out that God put out an impulse into the universe so that every entity, every cell in the whole universe is going to have this impulse *to be.*" He said, "Nobody will go to Hell, if they all have real being." And Satan said, "Gee, that is a problem. Let me think about this overnight."

The next day, the little imp comes in, and he sees Satan, not only having half the furnaces burning, he's now lighting up the rest of them. The little imp asks, "What are you doing? I told you that God put out this edict 'to be.'"

He said, "I know, but I added something to it. I added to be *good,* to be *famous,* and to be *rich.* See, I put a little tagline on it; now we'll get them all."

"To be" is what we need, but a tagline has been included. It's the equivalent of Kundabuffer. It becomes active. You're born with a very infantile being, and before anything real can take place, you start to have an education to be this, to be that, and that starts to create the illusion of being. We're educated to create this illusion of *being something,* and that's the contents of the centers. Certainly, not all; some contents are different and each center has its own content, and its own illusion of being; even our postures act as an "I am."

3.03 Q: Is one able to detect ego and work directly with ego?

JB: One of the machine's main fuels is ego; probably 85 percent of what drives me is ego. With a little less ego, maybe our whole life would be different.

3.04 Q: What do you mean when you say that real Work cannot be for personality profit or even for essence profit? Can you explain the idea that the result comes from the sincerity of the effort, not from the magnitude of the effort?

JB: According to the Enneagram, you could say that personality is based on the frequency of vibration of H192. You can say that man is a triad which includes false personality, which is H384, total illusion and personality; H192 which is education and formatory apparatus to a degree, what we've learned; but the third part of the triad of ordinary man is essence, H96. We live, mostly, between false personality and personality, between H384 and H192, with very little essence, H96. But we're very hungry for essence. We have a need for a relationship with it, unless it has died. I have seen people buy art for that. They're hard-nosed businessmen, who usually try to get a bargain, and suddenly they pay through the nose for a work of art. There's something about it they had to have. I saw these hard-bitten, what I call fork-tongued, buffalo-shooting businessmen come in, and be *touched* suddenly. It has to be real art, however, and there are certain artists that have something more objective in them; they're able to transmit a finer vibration.

The magnitude of the result doesn't necessarily come from the magnitude of the effort. I can feel a certain I-am-ness, the equivalent of having a permanent I for a moment. If you make an effort to search for the succeeding higher and you make an effort to maintain that, there will be another result entirely. There's nothing in life that *needs* consciousness. Consciousness will *help* you in life, but there's no *need* for it. If you're in a state of identification, the last thing that the I's that are identified want is consciousness. They don't want the light of consciousness. We need passive personality to evolve in the evolving triad. Active personality is the descending triad. You have to see and know the difference.

47

You need to maintain the effort of consciousness along with the idea of active personality and passive personality. If you maintain the effort for a certain period of time, you may see the posture you're in: your shoulders are up, you have this expression on your face, all artificial; you're leaning over and you can't get your head back, and you're nodding, even though you think they're full of shit or you don't agree with anything, you're still nodding, like one of these bobblehead dolls on a car dashboard. And you see in the emotions you're just trying to impress this person. You *feel* at that moment and you see how mechanical it is but the personality can't take the light, and suddenly it's gone; it hides. Depending on how deeply I see it, those I's disappear and could even be gone forever, according to how deep their roots are. This kind of seeing enables me to get to passive *Do*, which is receptive personality, and the I's that wish to evolve that wish to help. These I's have the right education and aim, and they're for the Work. They're not part of an unhealthy ego; they're running now on another fuel, a fuel needed to get to essence; for that moment, you're free of active personality. Through this kind of seeing you realize that you've been dragged through your life, in the best times as well as your worst times and all the times in between, by this claw that's been around your neck; that claw is active *Do*, active personality. It's dragged you down the path of least resistance all your life. Suddenly, at the moment you see that, you realize that. It's still not essence, but a freedom appears. But in the next moment, active *Do* imitates passive *Do*. You have the self-remembering look. You're still really close to that state of relaxation, but you're not sensing yourself anymore; you've now got active *Do* imitating passive *Do*. It's a situation that one has to see and recognize over and over again.

I need to work for a different consciousness, for a different reason, because drop by drop I deposit a finer vibration in me, which is accumulated. It may be at a certain moment that when I make an effort, I make it from a much higher energy, and then the reconciliations are much higher.

Sometimes, if you bring a high enough energy, you just skip through the Enneagram to another part of the triad to the left side of the Enneagram; you reach it immediately. It's even possible you can see chief feature for a moment. This level of effort could bring you to *any* triad of the Enneagram, at any time. You could have an experience of the higher centers. I've had experiences of H6, and of H12. That's why I diagrammed the Enneagram the way I did. I began to understand what the characteristics of those notes might be.

3.05 Q: What is sincerity?

JB: Conscience is what we must aspire to. It begins with real remorse. I was told time and again I was practicing cheap remorse. I'd bring in my sob story and would be told this is cheap remorse. I was given special exercises by Mme. de Hartmann to be able to open to real remorse, but at that time I wasn't ready for it, and I couldn't understand why she gave me these exercises. I didn't have the right feeling. Later, I understood the exercises she gave me and was able to use them to acquire the right vibration of feeling. What we usually call "sincerity" is usually cheap sincerity or cheap remorse. Gurdjieff refers to this as a very big weakness. So, one must ask, what does it really mean to value consciousness?

Gurdjieff says, "Conscience is to the emotions what consciousness is to the mind." When he says conscience, he means objective conscience, that everyone in the world will feel the same. In one country, everyone will have the same morality, but if you go to a different country, those same actions and thoughts may be considered immoral. Yet, there is also an objective morality that has been implanted within all of mankind but has been buried. Personality is a lie based on the illusion we'll live forever. We think that we're the center of the universe. Even the galaxy is too small for personality. It can't conceive of death. That's why when one sees deeply enough one sees that everything underneath is fear. Personality knows it is a lie and that it will die. So it bends over backwards to act and feel the opposite. Otherwise, how could we do what we do? In fact, everything we do, we do as if we were going to live forever. How not to lie? This is interesting because as you become more essential, you start to see this unconscious lying. You start to correct yourself in conversations because you see yourself exaggerating. As you become even more conscious this changes, but it is not a question of mechanical lying or mechanically telling the truth. If you are able to consider externally, then if you need to lie, you lie, if it is all for the good of the person and yourself.

Gurdjieff spoke about clever sincerity and stupid sincerity. When you are stupidly sincere, people will walk all over you. There are predators in life that are looking for this sincerity and will use you. This means you can't be sincere with just anybody. I realized that I had been stupidly sincere most of my life. Up to that point I had not been really sincere with anybody, and it was my responsibility to know with whom to be sincere and with whom not to be sincere. I found I was able to have friends with whom I didn't have to be sincere. I knew they would use me if I showed weakness, so I was strong with them. There were other people whom I call triers. I was able to open my heart to them, and I was able to be friends with them as well. It is like the difference between inner considering and outer considering. Bringing clever sincerity and stupid sincerity into life changed my personal life a lot. It solved the problem of trying to be sincere without getting stepped on.

3.06 Q: What is active personality as opposed to passive personality?

JB: One of the very important moments in my Work life was when I picked up Nicoll's *Commentaries* and read an extraordinary statement: "We have been taught that the evolutionary octave starts with a *passive Do*." I was stunned, because you would think it starts with an active *Do*. But I realized, of course, the ray of creation is a descending octave which begins with an *active Do*: the higher meeting the lower and becoming the middle, an involutionary octave. A force can be either passive or active in the moment. If you are in the descending, involutionary octave, it could be a passive or active force which is descending. The evolutionary octave is the active force. The Absolute descends and creates the universe, including organic life on Earth, the moon, and beyond, then returns. The universe is maintained by energies; I don't know what the reconciling force would be in relation to these two giant octaves, maybe world maintenance. Descending becomes more and more mechanical.

Returning against that descent is very different. In an evolutionary movement it has to become more and more conscious.

50

The energy becomes more and more refined. To me, the Enneagram reflected the evolutionary movement and the octave reflected the involutionary movement. The evolutionary octave is about enlightenment. That got me thinking. It all made sense. It is easy to think that passive is bad. The idea of being passive as a start to the evolutionary movement was a revelation. I started to see that my personality was neither receptive nor passive.

When you bring Work methods into your life you bring a real active force. And what does it meet? It meets another active force, personality, and the two active forces repel each other. How do we stay present, maintaining an attention? Even if I sense a part of my body, the next moment I'm gone. How do I maintain an attention long enough to see my personality and how it works? In *Beelzebub*, Gurdjieff says, "Holy Affirming, Holy Denying, Holy Reconciling, transubstantiate in me for my being." Our problem is that we have what I call an *un*holy denying which is active personality. It is necessary to transform active personality into passive personality in order to reconcile at essence.

Struggling against personality is like looking into the distorting mirrors at a Coney Island funhouse. Our centers are also distorted. Now, if we are rooted in a real body or real mind or real feelings, depending on the center we are working with, we can see more objectively. As we bring inner light, active personality is exposed, and it lets go and turns passive. Now I'm in a state of passive/receptive personality. Active personality, the grip that has dragged me through my life, has suddenly let go.

Passive/receptive *Do* is a wonderful state, but this is not my final destination. I now know the direction I am going in. I'm still trying to remember myself, following the indications of one of the representatives of self-remembering. Both forces exist. I'm present, I'm aware. I need to turn active *Do* H192 passive. Then the struggle is to bring the active force of the Work, H48, to passive H192, and through the law of triadic attraction, or self-tuning, to be reconciled at *Mi* H96; essence and can become receptive to a succeeding higher. In my view of the Enneagram, active *Re* H48 represents tasks or methods of a real teaching. In the beginning, this struggle is brought into my life by the meeting of two *active* forces repelling each other, active *Re* H48 and active *Do* 192. Only sustained effort to maintain the struggle between these two active forces will result in *Do* H192 becoming passive/receptive and thus becoming open to a succeeding higher, active force! When you reconcile at essence, *Mi* H96, the triad is completed, you then feel the joy of life, you love people who Work. It doesn't matter what you think of their personalities because you get by that immediately and you love them as brothers in the Work. We need more of this.

Essence is a state of love, where all three centers exist simultaneously—maybe not unified, but simultaneous. It's from essence that you can eventually cross to the left-hand side of the Enneagram, the next evolving triad. That's the first conscious shock where energies are transmuted and transformed into the much higher vibrations needed to feed our higher centers, to feed our real emotional center. This is lawful, a science. Unless you have those energies you are not going to sense the results of them! The trap is that if essence, after reconciling, becomes active to a preceding *lower* without making the proper effort to go further, I fall back out of the evolutionary movement, back into the involutionary movement, and right out of the Enneagram

We have to bring this demand for attention not just for the occasional Work fix or titillation of energy but for self-knowledge. Bringing Work methods to get self-knowledge, you suddenly see active personality for what it is and struggle to be free of it. If you're successful, you are at passive *Do.* But a few minutes later you can see active *Do* is imitating passive *Do;* you have that self-remembering expression on your face but you're not sitting straight and you're not sensing your body: personality is mimicking self-remembering; you've lost the connection with active *Re* H48 (your struggle or task) and your attention. I can maintain this struggle at passive *Do* like a preemptive strike, to prevent active personality from automatically imitating passive/receptive personality. I immediately need to find exact methods *before* active personality returns. I need to find a *new* active force! One example would be to like what it does not like. When we say "like what it does not like," what is "it"? It is *active* personality, my habitual strong likes and dislikes. I go against what active personality is attracted to at that moment. I use this to awaken; this struggle can bring me to a state of passive *Do*. If I'm asked to do something in work conditions, I do it to go against active personality, like work in a dirty basement, volunteer for the manure team, to like what it doesn't like. I went against everything that *it* liked. For example, years ago at Mendham we were supposed to pick up a large, heavy ladder. I saw that I wanted to take the light end, so I took the heavy end. Every moment there is an automatic inclination to do something in a way to protect oneself. We are never out of opportunities to go against personality.

Gurdjieff's aphorisms are all remarkable. Another one is "Remember yourself, always and everywhere." We know about "always," but what about "everywhere"? Are we willing and able to bring these efforts into the dark and hidden parts of our life? It reminds me of the Mullah Nasr Eddin story, where Mullah is searching under a lamppost for his key. A friend comes along and asks him what he is doing. Mullah says, "I'm looking for my key." After both look for a long time his friend asks, "Are you sure you lost it here?" Mullah says, "No, I lost it over there." His friend asks, "Why are you looking here?" And Mullah responds, "Well, there's more light here." We think that's a funny story, but think of it in relation to our observation. Do we look in the dark or do we always try to look in the light? It's much easier to stay with your eyes closed, dreaming that you're looking. We want objective self-knowledge. We need it.

3.07 Q: Would you say that when someone is in experimentation, that person can't use active personality anymore?

JB: I would say at that state, active personality would not exist. But he could use all those parts that active personality was based on. He would have a grown essence; personality would be passive, at the service of essence, a real state of quiet mind.

Associations are one of the greatest gifts that God has given man; however, when they're the active force they're horrible, but they can be incredible servants. In real thought, you have to be in quiet mind for long periods of time. It's very rough terrain to get to quiet mind, because the conceptual I is in the way of it. The most difficult thing is to sacrifice conceptual I, to die to that. That brings fear like you can't imagine since you *are* the conceptual I. Fortunately, if you're on the right track, it's not a long chasm; it's deep, but it's bridgeable. You get by it quickly if you maintain the right Work.

So it's not about whether one uses active personality later on because active personality is corrupt in the sense of I's that still rule. This is another reason to always go through interference for a while, because if you go through too quickly and you get to participation before you're ready, some of those I's which would have been eliminated will instead steal the energy that should go to participation. And if you haven't really gotten to passive *Do*, if there's still some active personality participating, those I's will steal that energy and inhibit going further. If you've been along the path, you know there are many traps and you experience them. The Enneagram is *so* important; it's what can keep you safe and on the path, and eventually it can be a teacher to a large degree.

One night, two mice were playing
on the rafters in a barn when,
becoming a little too exuberant and
careless, they suddenly toppled off and fell
into a large bucket filled with milk.
They kept swimming around desperately
until they realized their situation was hopeless
and they would never get out.
At this point one of the mice gave up
saying, "It's useless to keep swimming,
we have no chance."
He stopped struggling,
sank, and drowned.
The other mouse kept swimming anyway
until he was so completely exhausted
that finally, with one last stroke,
he passed out.
Later, he awoke and found himself
lying on top of a bucket of butter.

"I'm in a different world, different set of values when I'm free of considering and lying, a world I need to start to inhabit."

4

CONSIDERING

4.01 Q: What is considering? What is the difference between internal considering and external considering? And what is the work of freeing one from considering?

JB: Gurdjieff said identification with people "needs its own designation because it's so big," and he called it internal considering. In my own Work, I discovered that there are three basic kinds of internal considering. The first type is to think, what an idiot I made of myself yesterday; it's the past.

The second kind of considering is depicted in a famous old *Mutt and Jeff* comic strip. In one, Mutt was going to Jeff's house to borrow a screwdriver. On his way there he said to himself, "He's not going to loan me the screwdriver. He's going to give me some excuse. I'm going to go there for nothing," and on and on and on! Finally, Mutt arrives and knocks on Jeff's door, when Jeff answers, instead of asking to borrow anything, he yells, "You can keep your goddamned screwdriver, we're not friends anymore," and walked away! It is considering about the future, fears and anxiety over what's going to happen and again, negative imagination.

And then there's the third, considering in the moment: I take a certain posture and I don't realize it; I'm leaning forward nodding my head. I have had experiences of finding myself in a posture that my personality thought it had to maintain for somebody I didn't even know, or for a boss, or whomever. Sometimes I found myself frozen and couldn't even move. But even for someone who works *for* me, someone I consider my underling, I would say to myself, "I don't want to make a fool of myself in front of this person; I must *act* like I'm their boss." You're considering all the time. So there's that kind of considering in the moment. Basically, there are three kinds of considering: the past, the future, and the present. And there are three different kinds of Work involved in that.

One of the things I found out is that the experience of struggle against and becoming free of considering brings an extraordinary sense of well-being, a very high state. How do we work on considering? I used to say if considering were an Olympic event, I would have won a gold medal. First, one must struggle against considering, *not to succeed,* but to see its power, that it has an enormous energy supporting it. When I give the task to struggle against the force of considering but not necessarily to succeed, everybody comes back saying, "Oh, I failed miserably. I couldn't change one bit!" But usually we don't even know we're considering because it's such a strong current and we're in it! The brilliance of Gurdjieff identifying such a trait is that nobody knows it exists; instead, we give excuses like "I'm being more honest"; but you're not being more honest, you're being weak! So when people struggle against it and report back, "I failed miserably, I couldn't change." I usually respond, "You didn't fail. You were asked to see the force of considering and you succeeded!"

There was a Buddhist in one of my groups who said, "This doesn't apply to me because I don't consider. Maybe because I'm Buddhist, I couldn't see one example. I don't consider at all." I said, "That's really very nice." I said, "Since you don't consider, you can get up and dance for us!

She asked, "What are you talking about?"

I said, "Well, you don't consider, you're free! So dance!"

"I couldn't do that!" she said

"Sure you could. You're not considering, so why not get up and dance?"

"No, no, I couldn't." She turned pale. And suddenly her eyes opened wide and she said, "So *that's* what you mean by considering. I have that all the time!" And it's true; she always had to act "properly."

People don't even know considering exists; they say things like, "I'm really being sincere." They're floating on that very strong current and they're giving it all kinds of other names, even saying how wonderful considering is.

First, if one struggles to see the force of considering, they reach the first lamppost. Then one struggles to go against small things. For example, if a waiter forgets to bring your water, you don't say to yourself, "Well, I really don't want the water." You don't say, "Waiter, you know you forgot to bring me the water. Could you please bring me the water?" Instead, you just let it go by hoping no one will notice. I see this all the time, and one can struggle against it. The energy is too strong to overcome, but you find a way to get around it. It's very interesting because you see again and again the tendency *not* to do something even when you can. It's a very strange movement; you don't go against the energy, you suddenly slide around it, but you see this movement and struggle against considering, and suddenly you find you *can* go against it.

A half-hour of struggling to go against a big identification brought me one of the high states of my life. I was at a party where I didn't know anybody, and I had to urinate. Of course, for a man to pee in a toilet bowl makes a sound, and he *knows* the people outside the bathroom door are going to hear the sound. I was in there a half-hour struggling, wondering why I shouldn't pee. I saw myself peeing to the side of the bowl, you know, to silence it. You know, there are Japanese toilets that play a variety of sounds while you pee—bird calls, music, and rushing water— all to cover up the sound. But I said to myself, "Everybody knows I'm in here peeing. I mean, what's wrong with peeing in the toilet?" I said, "I'm going to do it." Now, that's considering. For a half-hour people knocked on the door and I said, "Not yet." I was determined not to leave that bathroom until I'd urinated, and finally, I did it. Before that, I didn't know anybody at the party and was ill at ease. But I walked out in total command, and I became the center of attraction there because I went into such a high state. Think of it, from *overcoming* considering about *peeing* I went into a high state! That showed me the power of going against considering, that was a struggle *against* it. Usually we *slide,* finding a way to move around it, but sometimes through our struggle something in us is freed, and we go right past it.

The next stage is to do something in front of people. You're nervous as hell, inside you're trembling, but outwardly, you could succeed and you could look calm. I once gave a talk at the Morikami Museum in Florida. The week before was a whole week of worrying, of anticipating with dread that I was going to be in front of this group and make a fool of myself. Not only was it in front of 120 people who were mostly retirees who weren't going to understand anything I said, but also the whole Boca Gurdjieff group was there and that worried me more. What if I give a bad talk? And that was the first breakthrough, where I had no fear, no anxiety, and was able to hold an entire audience in the palm of my hand, for an hour and twenty minutes. I found an energy that was so powerful because I was free of considering; a wonderful thing to be able to speak without those weights, that anxiety and nervousness.

Those are the stages; first you struggle in order to sense its force, usually with smaller things, but it could be a big thing one day. You don't know. You never know when you'll have a result; you just need to struggle. You just concentrate on making that movement, make a commitment. In order to go against considering, you have to remember yourself a lot. You're struggling to be present. But even when you're free of considering, if you're not remembering yourself, what are you free for? Remember, in the Enneagram, you always have to be free for a succeeding higher. When you're free you could be at the service of a higher nature, or it could be things in life. Gurdjieff always brought, "What's the next step?"

With external considering, you try to see what people need. And if you see what they need, you're at the service of that. Somebody's very unhappy and you know that they're lonely, so you make yourself available more than you usually would; it's not that you're doing it because of inner considering or to get rewards, because sometimes you make an effort and they turn on you. Don't expect gratitude because your heart will be broken. *You have to do it for consciousness*.

4.02 Q: Is external considering what Gurdjieff meant in

saying that we have to consider in the Work?

JB: Gurdjieff said we have to externally consider *more* with people in the Work because we're all essence brothers; we're more than essence brothers, we're brothers in consciousness. When you're in a lower state you can't bear the people in the Work because of personalities. When you're in a better state, you love everyone in the Work. "One has to externally consider people in the Work more." It requires a respect for the Work and a very special effort. Now, I may not be able to do it in my ordinary state. It's similar to a task that's given in the Work, of doing a job *consciously*; to do this job *as if* one *were* conscious. There's no greater shock than seeing one's unconsciousness in trying that task. When you try to do something as if you were conscious, you get such an impression of sleep, you start to see that you're considering internally, that you're expecting others to meet *your* requirements. This is why second line of Work is very important because one of the principles of second line of Work is that I don't come with requirements and I do what's asked of me. I come to receive a higher: whatever it is that takes that place, even if I'm cleaning a bathroom, that's the higher; I serve that; it's the equivalent. How can I serve God if I can't even serve a urinal?

4.03 Q: It's hard for me to be sincere enough to know whether I'm about to do something because I'm considering internally, or I really wish to externally consider someone else. For example, am I helping someone because I'm considering internally (I don't really want to be there, and I actually have something much more important to do, but I'm considering too much to tell them), or whether I am doing it for consciousness and am able to make that sacrifice and actually help them? It's often hard for me to tell whether I'm internally or externally considering when I help someone. For instance, it might seem like a sacrifice or effort to really help someone, but maybe I am just afraid to say no.

JB: How do you know you're considering? It's usually an emotional attachment which could be a weakness in the emotions; my reaction is to justify it. This is why you're working on presence. It's only you *being there* to see both sides. Usually I'm with one or the other; if you're a little more awake, you see that I have an I that says,

"What in the world am I doing this for? I'm stupid," and another I is saying, "Oh, I'd better do it because it would look bad." Or maybe it can't help itself; it's got to do it. Now, if I can be in front of that, that's what presence, is. One will win, but nothing can tell you which is which except your being present. And presence is like a third force. It's the reconciled result of a triad of struggling to be awake. It's like the middle, and then, if you can see what is true, maybe you can work against considering at that moment.

4.04 Q: Is it somehow related to wrong work of centers?

JB: Yes, because it's emotional when I usually should be physical or mental. As Gurdjieff said, it's so big that it deserves its own category. *It's with people.* Wrong work of centers could be anything; it doesn't necessarily have anything to do with people. But considering is *only* concerned with people, except you can even consider a dog, you know; you slip in front of a dog, you try to make it look intentional. You even consider people that aren't there.

"I don't move; I let the energy move. This is a practice. I surrender to the energy. I allow it to move. I am the vessel for this movement. If one could be like that in action, it will be done. That would be the right work of centers; the energy has to be put before the question 'Who am I?'"

5

UNITY

5.01 Q: Can you talk about the Work which relates to how the energies unify the centers?

JB: Gurdjieff brought us a picture of the dichotomy of the human structure. He tells us that the higher centers are already *fully* developed, but our ordinary minds, or brains, are so out of tune, out of relationship, and work with lower, incompatible energies so that they can't relate to each other. We have to quicken our lower centers; it's only *that* quickening which will allow us to relate to finer energies from the higher centers.

All of us have had experiences of being in states with finer energies, and people even have states of bliss; one gets very high on these energies, and then they go. These kinds of experiences could be a trap for many people. The memory of those higher states may be enough to give some people the illusion that they're still connected or that they are enlightened. But these states never stay, and I'm back to the center of gravity of my level of being.

If I work on myself, higher energies will come. It could be something very high, who knows? God gets into you, and the energy animates you for a minute, but then leaves and you're without it. If I don't have a vessel for higher energies, then, like a lightning bolt, they will go through me and into the Earth. I'm a conductor for something very high, but nothing remains. We need a *vessel* for these high energies. In the Work, the idea is not just change of state, but change of being. My work is the struggle that will allow this accumulation of astral matter that could bring me a higher body. Then the higher energies can be helpful to me; otherwise, they go through me and are gone. How can something be kept behind? How could we activate the law of three, the law of Triamazikamno, in relation to these higher energies? According to this law: the higher blends with the lower in order together to actualize the middle, and thus to become either higher for the preceding lower or lower for the succeeding higher. Let's start with the higher blends with the lower to actualize the middle. People often look to retain the higher, or go after the higher again. We dream about the higher; people have high experiences; they stay with the memory; they imagine that the state still exists. I usually burn up the energy that comes. But what is this middle? This middle is the result of the coming together of two forces. We need a vessel to store that result. If I wish to have change of being, I need something that retains the middle, which could be mine. I need for my being to increase its vibratory rate, to be more vivid. Right now, we look inside ourselves, and there's *no* being, there's *no* vibration of life. What would it mean to have a vibration of life that circulates and stands in front of anything? I don't lose myself. The vessel eventually becomes a Kesdjan body or an astral body.

It's through the daily grind, the daily Work, that I start drop by drop to deposit this very fine vibration in my vessel, and it may be only be a drop, but they add up. There starts to be a receptive quality to these energies.

5.02 Q: What is the work which is aimed at creating this vessel?

JB: In *Life is Real, Only Then When I Am*, Gurdjieff brought us an exercise in which he speaks about the coating of a higher body through the breath, the exercise of I am, I can, I wish. Mme. de Salzmann brought another aspect to your question of sittings, in which the aim was first to understand why I do the exercises, and to understand the meaning and the aim of what I'm doing, and then to bring the attention out of the path of least resistance. The attention of a real man is a representation of real will, and this requires what Gurdjieff calls "self-remembering." It takes awakening. This attention has to come under a different authority

65

than my ordinary I's.

All vibrations exist at once. I need to become a receptor, receptive to a certain frequency of vibration. My problem is that I'm not on reception, I'm always on transmission! Even if I can become receptive, what do I hear? The equivalent of a rap station; the associative process is just turning because that's all I'm receptive to. We need to start to enhance and vivify the vibration of our lives, the vibration of the way I live, because the food of impressions is what allows the air octave to create this higher inner body. Through this approach to have a body that's receptive to my ordinary states, and to start to see myself, I see what's in the way of this vivification. I start to see all of the leaks that take my force. This struggle is what produces a vessel, drop by drop and day by day. The sittings and our work in life are both necessary. As I plug the leaks and let go of the waste, I start to see places I need to go in the sittings, which have very narrow openings. I'm normally carrying so much baggage that I can't even *see* the openings; and even if I do see an opening at that moment, when I'm sitting, there's no way for me to get through because I won't let go of these structures of personality. If I work on myself during the day, observe myself, the baggage starts to erode; through the observation of bringing a light into my life and finding that I can suddenly enter new, sacred places in myself, it's like a new world.

The mind is noisy; it's turning; it's thinking; it's associating. My feelings; usually I'm feeling nothing, or I'm irritated. I start to investigate this. I look in my body and I don't find a real vibration of life; my mind, my emotions, my body are all noisy. But if I can go further there is a *void*, a place of complete silence, nothingness. My ordinary mind can't recognize this nothingness. The energy and nothingness are not related triadically; the emotions can't recognize it, and postures and tensions certainly can't recognize it. As the sittings become more advanced, I start to find by myself, or I'm given, ways to move into emptiness, a void, a space that has no I. This work is very difficult, to be in nothingness, right? And yet that nothingness is more intelligent and filled with a much finer energy. It's just that I can't perceive that energy now; it has a flow, a circulation, a resonance in the whole body, but I can't yet be aware of it. The first note of the octave of that resonance is silence, complete stillness. If you have this experience and suddenly you *can* find these places in yourself, you can be freer and larger than your personality, even your essence. Occasionally in life, your features, even your chief feature, fall away and you're free of them for a period of time. You can have moments here and there. You can enjoy them, but you don't quite understand the results or what to do next triadically.

I discovered that certain tensions in my breathing stopped me from intentionally going deeper into myself. I was given certain indications by Mme. de Salzmann, like "If you can't get there from above, try going from below, or from the side." These kinds of exercises helped me have these experiences, but these are changes in state, not being. When I returned to my level of being and its ordinary state, I would again find that I was blocked by tensions in my breath. And as I faced that more and more, I suddenly found that my whole stomach and abdomen would start to vibrate, not a little shake, but a violent vibration. I mean, if people looked at me, they'd see my abdomen and stomach were going out and in. It was frightening at the beginning, and what I realized was that the vibration was the letting go of these tensions, but I would start to let go and at the same time couldn't let go of them. Slowly, as I experienced this *it* let go, until suddenly it was gone. Then I found I could enter these places a little easier; still difficult, but I could enter a little easier.

In the void, you're faced with the question "Who am I?" How do you sacrifice your conceptual I, your emotional I or your sense of I? It's you *looking* at this "place." One day there will have to be a shift because that's where the true I is, where the true Garden of Eden is, and we've been exiled from it. I think that's the real meaning of what it means to be expelled from the Garden of Eden because we ate of the Tree of Knowledge. What is the Tree of Knowledge? One would expect that God would say, "Thank you, I've been waiting for you to eat that apple for the last two thousand years. You've just been hanging around the garden. I finally had to convince a snake to tell you." Why wouldn't God want us to eat of the Tree of Knowledge? We've been expelled from it, exiled into our minds, emotions, and bodies. This void is the center of gravity of the true vessel. The return to it is very difficult because we've accumulated so *much* baggage in our personality that our ordinary centers can't receive this sacred energy. The Work must become the active force that I bring into my life, and the methods of the Work bring moments of change of state. This emphasizes the day-by-day struggle, not necessarily results, the little efforts, the moments in which I've committed to something a little more. That is the Work towards adding a new center, the void that's really sacred and can receive the sacred. We must find this new place that will unite the centers and create a vessel.

5.03 Q: What is the meaning of the Zen term no-mind?

JB: The elimination of associations and formatory thoughts and vivifying the energy of the mind—I found out how to come to the state called in Zen no-mind. This state can last for very long periods. There is a certain path, and a certain time for bringing this effort, which is like the Dark Night of the Soul.[1] Poem from Spanish, sixteenth-century Roman Catholic mystic, St. John of the Cross. When you work this way you are actually eliminating conceptual I, you actually feel the terror of dying to it. It's frightening at that moment when you're losing your associations and conceptual thoughts. Then, I found it isn't a big gap; it's like a deep chasm, the great darkness of fear, but it's not wide. I found that this energy will carry you right past this interval. I used to have minutes of no-associations, then hours of no-associations; later, days and weeks. It was in this state of no-mind that the development of my new interpretation of the Enneagram came, and I think I even became receptive to the higher intellectual center at times. With this new relationship with my mind, I was able to understand in a new way.

The results of vivifying these energies came with even more experiences, such as seeing chief feature. I believe I did see chief feature, and chief feature dissolved. This is why I feel that what Gurdjieff said about seeing chief feature for oneself is very different than the dangerous practice of telling people what their chief feature is. Because people can hear what it is, know it, but never get rid of it. It's more important for a person to get rid of chief feature than to know about it. Having someone else tell you about your chief feature can even stand in the way of getting rid of it, because it's the wrong part that knows of its existence. If chief feature knows about itself, it's not going to allow you to make the right efforts to get rid of it!

5.04 Q: Regarding self-remembering, we heard you describe a work on an octave from the Enneagram: the sensation of I to the feeling of I. Can you elaborate on this?

JB: In the food diagram, Gurdjieff describes how the transformation of energies takes place up to a certain point with mechanical shocks, and then everything stops. To keep the transformation going, the first *conscious* shock is needed, and the order is very important. He describes this as bringing self-remembering to receiving impressions.

In the Enneagram we see that we have to start with the active force because the passive force has been corrupted and has the *illusion* that it is active. If I begin with the impression, the mind will dream that it's taking in the impressions rather than being a vessel. However, impressions should come through the mind and join the body. According to Kenneth Walker, Gurdjieff said, "The mind's function is to receive impressions; that it's an apparatus to bring in impressions." Practically, it really begins more with the sensation of I, a work brought by Mme. de Salzmann. It was very difficult, and at first I couldn't understand what it could mean. You have reminding factors. I remember a task that was given; you pick a doorway, and when you go through it you want to have the sensation of I, including the sensation of I-am-ness, which is not just I having sensation. But now you are trying to have a vibration in which you add the secret name of God, I Am That I Am. You are adding something from another world. It was very difficult but we worked on it, we struggled and failed, and then came a moment with a sensation of I-am-ness, which coexisted with the real vibration of the body. You work, maybe a year, on the sensation and evolution of I-am-ness, and then you start bringing work on the feeling of I through the struggle with reminding factors.

To digress for a moment, the Work was always with reminding factors. Once, in the days of the Prieuré, a child disobeyed special rules and was punished. The mother took him to a room off the main salon and one could hear the spanking. And then the door opened and the child ran off, pointing to his derrière, crying, "Reminding factor, reminding factor." It was part of the life there. I learned about reminding factors through working with Mme. de Hartmann, Mrs. Sutta, Christopher Fremantle, and Mme. de Salzmann. They always brought reminding factors. It was important that tasks and reminding factors were always done as given.

Mme. de Salzmann once brought a task to remember yourself and have the sensation of "I am" at 10:00 AM and 2:00 PM. I brought to the group that I tried every hour. Mme. de Salzmann seemed angry: "What do you mean you tried every hour? That was not the task. That could be harmful." I explained that since I didn't do the task all week and the meeting was tonight, I decided to do it every hour up to the meeting. And such a smile broke out on her face. She said, "To do it every hour was not the task. It is not the Work." I later understood that doing a particular task more frequently instead of at the designated times promotes the disease tomorrow because if I don't do it this hour, I will do it the next. But if you only have one or two hours to do it in, you can't escape it: I missed it; I was asleep; and the shock comes! Then the next time you realize that to be present at that precise hour, you have to be present earlier or to be present all morning. I remember once seeing that in the morning as I walked out the door, I got identified with a thought, and I knew that if I stayed with that thought, I would never be able to make the time; and because I saw that, I was able to interfere with it. It is an interesting reminding factor, but within certain limits. The use of reminding factors is a science. Just as a task is like a surgical instrument, each time you fail something is deposited. You learn something and understand at a certain moment what work you really need because you struggled and failed. The same thing with the feeling of I. We worked on that even longer; it's very elusive.

Once Mme. de Hartmann gave me a series of exercises in which I had to visualize terrible things I did to my mother. I said, "What do you mean by terrible things?" And she said, "Try to visualize a time when you made your mother cry." Do you know how painful that is? The task was to sit down for a period of time, collect myself, and then try to feel real remorse. Moments when as a child I made my mother cry came back to me. Sometimes I wept, but most times all this visualizing was water off a duck's back. I asked her, "Why are you giving me this?" And she said, "Maybe it is not for now. Maybe for the future." Later, when I was working with the body and the energy of the mind, those exercises became very important. They weren't completely what I needed, but they moved me in the right direction. Real remorse is not that common or easy to acquire.

We have to learn to separate consciousness from our functions, from thinking, feeling, and sensing; that is why we need this practice. I once thought that when we are born a light is given to us, and as we live we become identified with the shadows this light produces. And the question becomes: What happens to the shadows when the light moves on? That is a devastating question. This light could in reality be equated with real I; only real I can go into a place in me that is the Holy of Holies, where the center of gravity produces a materiality drop by drop. If our real I is to live on, consciousness has to be separated from the functions. In Solomon's temple there was the Holiest of Holies. The high priest alone could enter the room. Doesn't this represent something in us? A place where ordinary I's cannot go, only I-am-ness? The idea is that the higher can meet this receptacle and then something is produced that's mine. We can't go directly to the feeling of I, but it may come in time as a result of this work, from the sense of I to the feeling of I.

We start traveling on this journey from H96 to H48. The sensation of I becomes finer sensation, and at some point it merges into the feeling of I as I move *up* the inner octave. Every note has an inner octave of *Do* to *Do*. At one point in *In Search of the Miraculous*, Gurdjieff says that the inner octaves are very important but he never explains why. The action of the attention is mysterious; there is a science to it, and the Enneagram explains it, that the simultaneity of the attention opening to the two forces brings in another kind of consciousness. This could be what Mme. de Salzmann meant by "the look from above." You don't *become* the higher consciousness, but it *coexists* with the level you're on, though it is only with the simultaneity of the attention that this happens. The problem is that our attention moves back and forth so fast from one center to another that it appears simultaneous—but it's not. True simultaneity of attention is a very big thing. It demands an expansion that has been atrophied in us. If you are in the right order in yourself and are maintaining the lower and the higher, you will find that the impressions that vivify this resonance will come in because only the resonance is able to receive the impression that is sensitive enough; it is a very fine energy that's living in the whole body.

This is why Gurdjieff said, "Bring self-remembering to an impression." If you can remember yourself, then the impression is there for you. You don't bring the impression. And then there are many ways to take in an impression. We try to study self-remembering, but do we study how to take in an impression? Isn't that a work? If self-remembering is the internal octave from the sensation of I to the feeling of I, is there an internal octave of impressions ranging from my mind being partially blocked by good thoughts to quiet mind or no-mind where that impression could be received and open my awareness as a whole? Is it possible to be so sensitive as to be able to feel the impact of the impression?

5.05 Q: How can an interval be recognized? How can one stay in front of an interval? How can a shock be provided in order to take one past an interval?

JB: Early in our work, we experience intervals. There's an interval for a day or a week; maybe a year, or a decade. My life has a very big octave in which the intervals are gigantic. It's one thing, early on, to see and feel a tension based on a habit and struggle against it. These tensions only exist in the dark; brought to light, they're seen. I call them the leaves, but in the larger octave of our individual lives, the *intervals* are the roots. A very long work is the illumination of chief feature, the seeing of it, knowing it, and its elimination, which will enable me to go further.

If you start to understand how to deal with intervals, it's possible to save a lot of time. We need to recognize the taste of an interval. I'm at an interval and I don't know it; the symptoms are that the energy is gone, the impulse and interest in work is gone. I feel guilty. I feel self-pity. I make all kinds of plans: Tomorrow I'm going to really work twice as much. All this weighs me down, and I fall away from the interval.

We know there's a pendulumatic movement to our struggle in the work. When I struggle and make efforts, I start to move towards a better state and to receive richer impressions. I start to live more vividly. But at a certain point it gets a little too rich and something in me starts to pull in the other direction. I don't yet have a vessel to support the intensity of this kind of energy. I can't take any more impressions; the energy is too strong, and so it starts to pour out through structures like negative imagination, negative emotions, and dreams. I have a certain range in this pendulumatic swing. I'll go up to a certain point, and then I'll start to move the other direction and pour out energy, but I always come back to the center of gravity of my level of being. When I start to receive impressions in a bad state, a state of imbalance, something in me opens up and says, "I've got to work." I start making little extra efforts. I start struggling a little more, and drop by drop, I start to move back in the other direction. This pendulumatic movement defines my life, at least in the early years of my work.

With each movement of the pendulum, I need to keep the higher state a little bit longer, and if I can maintain the level long enough, my *being* will change: it will rise. Inhibiting the downward movement by a little extra struggle *at that moment* is a very big thing.

I can use the Work that Gurdjieff brought us with all its forms: group meetings, Movements, work in the moment, readings and discussions; they're second line of Work. All of these activities can supply shocks to get me past intervals. The problem is that when I come to an interval where one of these forms would bring the shock, instead of staying at the interval, I'm taken away. I once recognized I was at an interval, that this was the taste of an interval. I saw guilt and self-doubt come in, and I realized this negativity was pulling me away from the interval. I begin my work week coming from the group having renewed the focus of my energies. I feel that energy, that vibration from another level, and *if* I'm open, I'm fed. Then I go out into my life, and if I don't have another work activity, I feel the energy eroding, even running out at a certain point. But then it's time for another activity such as Movements that can replenish the energy.

Then every time I get to an interval, either the forms of the Work are there, or I put myself under a form of the work, like volunteering to work a day in the library or some other nonhabitual activity.

I discovered later, with the Enneagram, that active *Do*, passive *Do*, and reconciled *Do* each have different tastes, three absolutely different impressions. Active *Do* and passive *Do*, a world of difference; active *Do* is a descent, the Ray of Creation; passive *Do* is the evolutionary movement, the difference between heaven and hell, between dying like a dog and trying to die like a man.

Every vibration has a level of consciousness, of intelligence, and of time. We have to understand the vibration of *Do*, the vibration of *Re*, *Mi*, *Fa*, *Sol*, *La*, and *Si*. In the Enneagram every note *has* several characteristics. It has the note of the octave it is in, which determines where it is in the Enneagram and where it is in relation to what we're trying. It represents an active, passive, or reconciling force, which means the direction it's going in. If it's active, it will be descending; if it's passive/receptive, it has the possibility of opening to a higher force and ascending; if it's reconciled, it will bring a sense of wholeness and then turn either active or passive depending on the influences. In other words, the vibrational rate, or the hydrogen involved, determines the level of consciousness and especially the value system. Without understanding this, one will never understand intervals or be able to get past them intentionally.

Personality has a very different vibration than essence, a different value system than essence, a different tempo. It even has a different body. Everyone must learn this taste for themselves. By knowing the taste of intervals, we can accelerate our Work, accelerate our change of state, and keep the pendulum higher for a longer time. This work will change our level of being.

5.06 Q: How can unification of the centers be achieved?

JB: I need the sensation of the different energies in the body. In the Work we start with the body: the energy of the body is available because the instinctive center has to protect and preserve the body to a certain degree. I need the sensation of my feelings, the energy of the emotions; we only know *those* energies through them

74

pouring out of us.

The mind is the most difficult. We're so identified with thoughts and associations and dreams that we don't know what the higher energy of the mind is; the taste of it. I don't have sensation of the mind. I either think or dream or I'm identified with it, and if I try to search for the energy of the mind, I'm thinking. But there is an energy of the mind and it's very important to eventually separate the contents of the mind from that energy. As we are, our centers don't usually work with the right energies. The contents of centers can never be brought together because they are too coarse and they are magnetized. Our attention is very susceptible to this magnetism, so when we're trying to work we see what pulls the mind. Likewise, we can be pulled to the contents of the emotions and the postures and tensions of the body. And sometimes emotional contents are in the mental center and in the body also. I have a thought that's glued to a certain feeling, that's glued to a certain posture, tied together in a cycle, what I sometimes call "three-centered gremlins."

This is the first stage of the Work on interference; one of its aims is to identify and to weaken the grip of the contents, and also on participation because in participation *any* contents stand in the way. When the Work brought by Mme. de Salzmann changed from interference to participation it brought a new possibility, but many people couldn't recognize it and rejected it. Others felt this didn't come from Gurdjieff because they had never worked with him in that way. Surprisingly, many of the group leaders rejected it. Later we found out that Gurdjieff did work this way, but only with his oldest pupils. The younger, "responsible" people, of whom I was one, seemed to take to this work of participation which involved centering very seriously.

The real aim of this work on participation is to bring you to another place in yourself that's *not of the centers*; an objective place in us that can be an active force in relation to all the three centers, like a refuge. That may be what is meant in Buddhism when speaking about taking refuge in the Buddha. In Judaism, the Temple of Solomon held the Holiest of Holies, the room that only the high priest could enter. This may be symbolic of what could be in us. We can have a place like that in us, but as we are now, nothing in us could enter such a room. We don't have the Holiest of Holies in us. We don't have that high priest anymore. We have to start to develop this place within ourselves, a new center of gravity. Mme. de Salzmann, quoting Gurdjieff, said that unless we develop this new center of gravity in a certain place in us that the centers can't go to, *no further Work is really possible*. Then she went on to describe how, if that center of gravity *is* developed, the energies of the centers can become unified.

We have the Devil working against us with the help of the centers. Contents are parasites; they eat up the energy of the centers. They have no energy of their own. The more content I have, the less energy I have. I talked about the force of triadic attraction, how the descent of the ray of creation materializes the universe. It works against consciousness, keeps us asleep so that we serve it. Without our being awake, nature takes everything. Contents pull us away from our aim, our path; yet at the same time, they may be our salvation. If you wake up, you can start to give the ray of creation *only* what it needs. You don't have to give it everything. The same triadic attraction between forces that works against us in the ray of creation now can be an extraordinary help in the *evolutionary* octave. There are also forces for evolving; in fact, without these forces, nothing can be done. My I's will never unify me; it's this triadic attraction that is my only hope, and will work; "it" cannot not work! It's a law of the universe. If I can start to learn how to discover and occupy this new center of gravity, and at the same time separate the contents from the energy, the energies of the centers can come together because these energies naturally are attracted to each other.

I believe this is truly the secret oral teaching of Gurdjieff, an initiation into a way of working, the real beginning of the Work. The attention has to open to two forces; part of my attention has to be on the materiality of this new center of gravity and on the three centers unified. Unity means the unification of the center of gravity where a real I can exist with the centers. First the mind and the body come together: the feelings act as the reconciling force to complete this triad, and this reconciled force must then become the passive force in this larger triad. It can then be reconciled into an astral body. I saw

76

this whole picture as an absolute, exact science in myself.

5.07 Q: How can I go against my tendency to go in just one of these directions?

JB: Well, look at it this way; this is a way of working on all three centers. The idea of the Fourth Way is the balancing and the unification of the centers. It's a shortcut. The way of the fakir is to develop will, starting with the body; the way of the monk is to develop will starting with the emotions; and the way of the yogi is to develop will starting with the mind.

The reason it's so important to be in a group is because if you're left on your own, you'll go down the path that you have an affinity for. That's also why I don't trust groups without a group leader because each person will only go down the path that they have an affinity for. Years ago, when I played a lot of tennis I used to notice certain things. I knew a man who had a very good forehand and a terrible backhand. He would come out on the court and he would get a ball-serving machine, and he would hit five hundred forehands and then go away. I'd be on the next court and I'd think, "Why isn't he hitting five hundred backhands? This is not what he should be practicing." I saw that people would only practice their strongest points. It's similar in the Work. For certain people, the intellectual part is the only thing that interests them. I once commented about somebody that he loves the ideas but hates the Work. What I meant by the Work is struggle with the body and the emotions, or work on sensation and feeling, second line of Work or third line of Work. It's the balancing and unification of the centers that's important. That's why second line and third line of Work are so important, where we get opportunities to work on different parts of different centers. With observation of centers, you start to see the wrong work of centers. You can't avoid working on all the centers if you're working on a right path, second line of Work, the Work ideas in action with the right people.

"Start to understand by taste the laws that apply to vibrations and a relationship between frequencies."

VI

SACRED LAWS

6.01 Q: Can you talk about your understanding of the law of three and how one can make that law practical? Also, regarding your law of triadic attraction: What do you mean by that?

JB: What is called empty space in our universe is filled with vibrations. And everything in the universe relates triadically. I believe that the law of three forces, the law of Triamazikamno, is the basic law of the universe: "the higher blends with the lower in order together to actualize the middle, and, thus, to become either higher for the preceding lower or lower for the succeeding higher." It is the motor that *causes* movement.

Then the law of seven, the law of Heptaparaparshinokh, describes *how* it moves. One movement is the descending, involutionary movement, which Gurdjieff calls the "Ray of Creation," the creation of the material universe. Everything becomes more and more dense, more and more mechanical, and comes under more laws. The other movement is the evolutionary movement, which I believe is the movement shown by the Enneagram.

All frequencies of energies relate to each other triadically, whether they move up or down. In *In Search of the Miraculous*, the forces are called active, passive, and reconciling (or neutralizing). In *Beelzebub*, Gurdjieff brings the formula as stated above and I believe that's the true formula and that it is as important to the spiritual world as $E=mc^2$ is to physics.

How then do we ascend in a world of mechanicality and with

an attention that only follows the path of least resistance? We can ascend by opening to something that could resist the preceding lower. I believe it is a consciousness that one could access, or it could appear as a result of effort, an "I-ness" that could turn the reconciled force to passive/receptive. You must be able to wait and resist the preceding lower, thereby becoming receptive to the succeeding higher, *which will appear if the right effort is made*. This process is what one must trust. The middle has only one influence on it *which is the preceding lower*. The succeeding higher is not yet there to influence you. If at that moment you bring a succeeding higher, you move to a very high energy. That is a *universal I* not an I that is attached to dreams, thoughts, or personality, or an I attaching to essence or an I attaching to a feeling of I-am-ness which is self-remembering, or even permanent I that still attaches to unity. This is an I attached to something outside of us; it is more universal, galactic. I have to open to this in order to resist the preceding lower. That means I have to allow that force to exist in me or have knowledge and being that could be receptive.

Try to divide your attention; no matter what the higher or lower is, you have to include both equally. Mme. de Salzmann's words were "50/50, that is your aim." It may start as 90/10 or 99/1, out of balance, but you struggle. I started to see that what I thought was simultaneity of attention to two forces was really jumping back and forth very quickly between one force and the other; but as you fail you start to observe more; you keep struggling and struggling, and then you succeed for longer periods of time, and suddenly for a moment it *is* simultaneous. You must be present; struggle demands vigilance so a higher consciousness can appear. Simultaneity of attention could also be *not struggling*, like the effortless effort, by which you learn to open in a new way. I discovered that if you can maintain that simultaneity for a moment you are able to see something extraordinary. When attention is 50/50, a new consciousness appears with your struggle on the level you are at. I equate this with what Mme. de Salzmann called in one of her talks "a look from above." The development of simultaneity of the attention has to be struggled with for a very long time. To make it practical I have to *accept* what I am at this moment, to bring a higher force to what I am now.

There is no such thing as a generic *Do*; there is *passive Do*, *active Do*, and *reconciling Do*. You have to come to the proper *Do*. If reconciling *Do* becomes active, it is going to descend; if it turns passive, it has the chance to move into an evolving octave. Understanding the law of Triamazikamno will make our work practical. Too much of our work is vague; we don't understand the role of tasks, that at any moment it is possible to evoke an ascending, evolving triad if I understand this law. What is the higher for me *now*? It is different for sleeping man, slumbering against the wall of an elevator, dreaming about something in the past and future. What would be the higher for him? Maybe sensing his left arm. And the higher for a saint might be to give up sainthood itself and open to God in a new way where the ego must be sacrificed.

I have to take an impression of myself, be present to myself right now to be aware of the sensation of my whole body, rather than just a part. Maybe my spine is not quite straight; I may have a mindset and mental picture of it being straight but maybe it's not really balanced. I have to straighten it, find a balance, and open the doorway to the sensation of the whole body. I can do that at any moment. The higher means to bring something *not of the personality*, not even of the essence, but the higher comes from the level of Man No. 4, from my *wish* for consciousness. I am not doing this to impress you—which is personality—or to feel good, or to be a better human being, or even because it is the moral thing to do. I am doing this because if I don't, I'll perish because there won't be consciousness or being. For whatever reason, something higher was planted in me that has meaning. Even though I may betray it again and again it comes back again and again. So I am here still struggling for consciousness. But a moment later I see my personality imitating my wish to work: I am not straight, I have lost the balance; a struggle is being done now by active personality imitating what would be passive personality, which could be receptive to a higher force, whereas active personality is not. This is the danger, the trap, and one has to recognize that trap.

My aim is not just to reach passive personality, although it is a wonderful state. In that state I feel free of my personality; I'm present in my body. But in that state I don't feel the sense of love that I would like to feel, or I have felt before and again; now I have to open to the mind. The triadic relationship is between the body and the mind, those two energies can relate. Then I am not thinking in an ordinary way, my mind is totally quiet. I'm a vessel for something that I trust. I bring this to the awareness of my body and I see that my attention is *not* simultaneous but is jumping back and forth, but I accept it; I experience it; I am struggling to be aware of the life of the body and the life of the mind that's keeping the evolving triad going. I don't know what the result will be. If I go for a specific result such as speaking better or to feel love, it won't take place. I don't know what will take place.

Now I see there is a suffering in me. I start to feel the activation of my emotional center. Again, I keep seeing how my attention jumps back and forth, without simultaneity of the attention I know there is something missing. I know that from experience. I feel the attention, at this moment. I'm trying now to be more aware. Maybe the entry, instead of being from the spot between the eyebrows, now has to come from the top back of the head, which is a way to open to the higher energies, just like the spot between the eyebrows is a way of opening to the associative mind and quiet it. I am now more centered in my body, trying to keep the vibration of the body alive, open to the sensation of the head or mind through the top back of the head. At the same time I have to risk it by speaking. This is wonderful because one always has to be willing to risk losing what one has. If I don't try, I'll go into dreams; the force will be only a single energy which will then go downwards. Risking means there will be a bigger demand on being present, and the risking becomes a succeeding higher for another triad. Now, I have to hear myself, sense the vibration in my voice. I can see it's so easy to lose this opening of the attention to both body and mind, but this is the struggle.

I need to have a toolbox of representatives of the higher, of self-remembering, which is what I need to bring to this moment, to what I am now. If I have only three tools, I am limited; if I have a

82

hundred, maybe even this is not enough. Group work gives me these tools and this is why we work together, not only using different tasks, but also using certain tasks for different reasons because sometimes one tool does many things. We need to use all of that to awaken to an I-am-ness, which is really at the heart of everything: the higher.

I believe scientists may discover these laws and the law of triadic attraction some day. The law of triadic attraction is going to answer many questions in physics which are now a mystery. Scientists don't understand this movement within.

"One of the very useful aspects of self-observation is that we start to see a creature filled with habits. As you go against them, you're challenging physical, emotional, and mental states connected to it."

7

WORK IDEAS

7.01 Q: How do self-observation and self-remembering relate to being-partkdolg-duty?

JB: Well, I'm very honored that you would ask me a question like that. Being-partkdolg-duty, or conscious labor and intentional suffering, applies on every level. I believe that conscious labor does involve taking the attention out of the path of least resistance. It demands an awakening whether it's passive *Do* or essence. If you do it for awakening, there's no personality profit or essence profit. The result would be evolutionary, more towards consciousness. But we don't maintain our efforts long enough. Efforts become mechanical too easily: I struggle for sensation, feeling, and thinking, and I believe that it's all accomplished. How do I maintain this effort? Sometimes we do a task for a certain length of time, like counting and sensing at the same time. This can have an action like putting a stick between the spokes of the spinning wheel: it interrupts my habits for a second; I get a glimpse of something true; and then I'm back asleep again. In the long run that's not enough. True self-observation hasn't appeared. We need to go further than that, and deeper.

In an evolving triad, we can't start with active personality. Most of the time we *live* in *active Do*, a descending octave. Personality as we live now is an active force: everything that we do in our life is from the point of view of I am, I exist, and I'm doing. I'm under the illusion that I'm the center of the universe. Gurdjieff is quoted by

Nicoll as saying that "the evolutionary octave begins with a passive *Do*." When I read that, it was very important to me, and one of the elements of my work on the Enneagram is based on this concept of passive *Do*. Gurdjieff's food diagram is one of the only places that I know of where he speaks about an evolving, transforming octave.

How do we get to passive *Do*? Our struggle needs to begin with bringing an *active* higher force, one of the methods of real Work like tasks, Movements, or work events. Active personality can't evolve. It relates to the lower by momentum. The ray of creation is a *descending* octave.

As we are, our attention is usually taken by active personality. So, one characteristic of being-partkdolg-duty is that the attention needs to be taken out of the path of least resistance. When I bring an active force from a struggle, such as a task, two active forces exist at the same time—active *Do* (my personality) and active *Re* (my struggle, the representative of self-remembering). Now two active forces exist, and what happens? I can't help but observe it. Active *Do* stands out; if I can maintain my struggle I cannot *not* see this artificial, ridiculous *slave* that's made up or invented. If you maintain your attention long enough while these two active forces are in opposition, you will see whatever *is* at that moment. This kind of self-observation and self-remembering are two sides of the same coin; one is an active force and the other is a result. In *Beelzebub* he speaks of visiting Gornahoor Harharkh and sees Harharkh demonstrate an experiment to artificially eliminate one force of the Okidanokh while maintaining just two forces. One of the results is the creation of a very bright white light. Isn't that what I've been talking about? The two forces are two active forces that produce this seeing. White light is the equivalent of seeing from another center. If personality is seen, it usually can't take the light and becomes passive/receptive. Passive/receptive *Do* needs a new kind of effort, which may even be more demanding. This is why one has to exercise and strengthen one's attention. You have to divide your attention between these two active forces. Active personality is still there, it has the attention. Some people will just try to do the effort, but they won't *see* because they *are* just one force, active personality. I want to sense my leg, but when I see my postures I don't want to see them. It's like closing your eyes to the bright light. Passive *Do*, passive personality is much more subtle, and it is through maintaining this division of the attention, with personality being passive, that you move to reconciled *Mi*, which is essence.

In this first triad of the Enneagram, one must use the effort to see what Gurdjieff calls the "leaves." In the next triad, maybe, you'll see the roots—much bigger features, or even my chief feature—and that's where real self-remembering in front of an impression comes in, a much more conscious level of Work, much deeper, with higher vibrations. It may be the exact same effort as the division of attention; the only difference being the level of hydrogens and the frequency of the vibrations.

Now that you have a background on self-observation and self-remembering, we can discuss intentional suffering. I once asked Mme. de Hartmann about suffering. She offered me a knife and said, "Cut your hand, and suffer if you wish. But that's mechanical suffering. I know that's not what you're interested in." Our ego suffers for a long time when we begin struggling with self-remembering. There's a separation, I and it. And what happens the next moment? One I is looking at a photograph of *it*, and that I suffers. The ego then comes in: "Oh God, how could it be this way? This is not the picture I have of myself." The emotions take my sense of I and go into reaction. But maybe I can see that what I call suffering is content, the suffering of the machine, the ego. Even the first moment of this kind of separation is very valuable because that will stay with you the rest of your life. That moment is real. Even if it was stolen very quickly by that little reactive I, that could be one's entire experience with intentional suffering. But if you can get past that point to a more objective level, you see it, and at that moment there's no reaction: you're not suffering; something is there that's absolutely objective.

This is why I say when there's real seeing there's no suffering in that reactive way. We need to *practice* intentional suffering. If you're in a higher state, or what Mme. de Salzmann called the look from above, and see objectively that this mechanical machine can't be different from its environment of accidental factors and is going through life the only way it can, that would *not* be suffering. Intentional suffering is not that. It's not reaction.

Gurdjieff spoke about conscious labor and intentional suffering as being on a much higher level, let's say, a much higher triad, where I have more unity and the energies are very fine. I need to bring an effort, not from cheap remorse but real remorse, or what Gurdjieff called the gnawing of conscience. And that can move me to real conscience. I used to come to my group meeting and Mrs. Sutta would say, "Cheap remorse." And I got that a lot at certain times. Conscience is something else; the remorse of conscience is a very high state. Gurdjieff said, "Conscience is to the emotions what consciousness is to the mind."

7.02 Q: What are buffers?

JB: In observing oneself, one has to first acknowledge that buffers exist. What's extraordinary about what Gurdjieff brought is that he delineated the characteristics that keep us asleep. Gurdjieff compares buffers to the couplings between railroad cars that reduce the shocks of the cars hitting each other from being transmitted to each other. For us, he said, buffers stop us from knowing our contradictions and feeling our contradictions. Buffers cut us off as we begin to feel a contradiction so we have a sense that everything is okay: we don't have to think about that. They interfere with the rising of conscience. They justify my behavior and the behavior of others.

All centers have buffers and they are very simple. A buffer could manifest as the raising of an eyebrow. It could be the phrase "So that's life." It could be a shrug of the shoulders or a mental phrase. If you can take in an impression of this repetitive phrase or your face as you raise the eyebrow, as the buffer comes in and connects itself to something lower, let's say self-pity, you can feel the contradictions. In feeling the contradictions, Gurdjieff says, "it will in you the rising of conscience." In our essence we have this extraordinary ability, or organ, of conscience. Gurdjieff also says that "conscience is to the emotions what consciousness is to the mind." Objective conscience is an extraordinary thing. If I can bear the suffering of the contradictions, something will change.

Buffers are very subtle, and one sees them by the struggle of sensing and maintaining a divided attention. You'll never see a buffer just by taking an inner snapshot, which is the beginning of observation. When you receive the shock of seeing yourself, you have to be present long enough to see how you digest that shock. If I sense my foot right now, there is a point where I see I have a certain amount of sensation. If I can keep my attention on my foot, the sensation becomes deeper, stronger. But I see I need to move my foot a little bit because it's not aligned: I move it, and my sensation is gone, and now I'm gone. The moment that you receive the shock of observing yourself, the buffer steps in. But by that time we're already reacting to the shock: we're analyzing the shock; or we're gone; or we're thinking, "How will I bring this to the group?" We move to another center in that moment and we lose our attention. We don't maintain separation or division of attention long enough, strongly enough, or consistently enough. But even if I lose my attention, the sensation can remain, like a fan when you pull the plug but the blades keep turning for a period of time. I lose my attention but then I come back; there is a rhythm to that. Sensation can keep me grounded. This is why we begin with the sensation of the body. Sensation alone, however, has its limits. What we call sensations of the flesh is the life of the body. There is another vibration, which I call succeeding higher H24. It has a much longer life when it becomes stronger, but it can also disappear very quickly. If I could find H24—it's very, very evasive, but that's what I need to carry into life, and it will help bring me back because I will *always* lose my attention; there will always be something that calls it. But if that vibration is there, my attention doesn't go far and I'll come back to it again. Provided I know what they are and if I'm able to maintain a seeing with another vibration, at first sensation, one center seeing another center and then with H24, seeing *all three centers*, buffers will start to appear.

7.03   Question: How do you respond to the following quote by Mr. Gurdjieff? "Every man has a certain feature in his character which is central. It is like an axle round which all his 'false personality' revolves. Every man's personal work must consist in

89

struggling against this chief fault."

JB: Chief feature causes my personality to be perceived completely the opposite of the way I see myself. I bend over backwards not to *be* it. It's the main ingredient of the structure of my personality. Chief feature cannot work in the light. This is why it's so hidden in us; it will only work in the dark. Mr. Gurdjieff described work on the chief feature by saying "the struggle against the 'false I,' against one's chief feature or chief fault, is the most important part of the work, and it must proceed in deeds, not in words. For this purpose the teacher gives each man definite tasks which require, in order to carry them out, the conquest of his chief feature. When a man carries out these tasks he struggles with himself, works on himself. If he avoids the tasks, tries not to carry them out, it means that either he does not want to or that he cannot work."

There is a difference between knowing your chief feature and getting rid of it. Seeing it is only part of the process of eliminating it. I believe that someone telling you your chief feature may even stop you from seeing it objectively and getting rid of it. It's my experience that if you really see chief feature, it dissolves. This is where I believe this vibration that I call hydrogen 24 is like a disintegrating ray. H24 is not triadically related to personality. So, when we are in H24 personality remains hidden. A real group leader should be bringing the resonance of hydrogen 24 to the group. He should be very aware of that vibration, and that's rare. It's an energy that I feel few know about. I realized this energy had appeared at all my important experiences.

I call chief feature, chief obstacle because in the work for unity there has to be another energy aside from the energy of the centers. The individual energies of the centers are not going to unite themselves. There has to be a separation in the Work. I learned that's just one I seeing another I is insufficient. You need to understand the difference between one I seeing another I and one center seeing another center; that's more objective. I know if I'm negative and I really bring sensation to my leg, that sensation couldn't care less about what my emotions are involved in; all the moving center wants to do is vibrate and expand. That's all it knows. It doesn't have "I hate this, but I like that." It's involved with pleasant/unpleasant! It may be neutral but it wants to expand, it wants to vibrate.

At any moment, the associative mind will be at the service of whichever center is serving the *body* or the *emotions*. This is the separation I was speaking about between these two energies, an active force and a passive force. One must be able to maintain this relationship of the centers through what I call the "law of triadic attraction" until they start to harmonize and eventually unify.

The chief obstacle to this harmonization is chief feature. Chief feature won't allow you to find your center of gravity from which this reconciling vibration can spring. You have to work on this. You struggle and struggle; this is a long work, not a work of a day, a week or a year. It's a work of a decade or maybe a lifetime. But when you try to get to this new place, you eventually need to see chief feature if you wish to really have real unification of the centers. That's a new center of gravity, the center of circulation of an astral body. As you strive to bring an attention to this work there is a point where you are aimed at that new center of gravity, but you can't get there. So what happens? You start to see everything interferes with that movement: postures, tensions, the way we breathe. You have to separate consciousness from associative thought. If you work on yourself, there are times when you are free of chief feature, but in general, you always return to your level of being.

All the centers are magnetized by content, like you magnetize a nail. This new center of gravity does not have magnetism; it needs gravity. In space, anything that's material has gravity: it attracts. This idea is not for right now; it is for after you see yourself and free yourself from the leaves, when you are working on the roots. This is when you are not trying to have a representative of self-remembering but to have *true self-remembering*.

7.04 Q: How does one recognize being in front of an interval?

JB: Another thing that was stressed when I came into the Work was that eventually you had to know the *taste* of every note of the octave. *Do* has a certain taste and characteristic ring in us. *Re* has its characteristics and *taste*, etc. The same thing with intervals: they have a certain taste. The real knowledge of intervals, not intellectual knowledge but the *taste* of intervals, is very important. We need to have many experiences of being in front of intervals. Often, what happens is that I don't know I'm at an interval. The result is that I feel guilty; I feel I can't work. When I start to feel self-pity or guilt and the frustration of the interval, I often fall away from the interval and become emotional. The shock comes, but I'm not at the interval anymore. My picture of myself has changed according to how I view myself in that moment. And one must start a new *Do*, which is actually more difficult than getting by the interval in the first place. I often feel like Sisyphus. The work is constructed in such a way as to provide shocks up to a certain point to get you past intervals.

Once, when I was with Mme. de Hartmann, I saw something very clearly in myself. For the next six months, whenever my associations brought me back to that impression, I felt organic shame. Instead of reacting, I was able to accept the impression of this organic shame rather than buffer up, or justify it. I had to suffer the interval. Seeing this and knowing what it was, it lost all of its force and action upon me. What I had seen was so clear that it brought me past the point I was at, and I changed! It was like a *Si-Do* shock. I went past the interval to a new octave. The next time I saw her, I found I was past the interval and I was able to have a different relationship with her.

In general, with all of the different forms, the Work is constructed so that the shocks are available to help you pass the interval. The trouble is we don't *stay* at the interval, *taste* the interval, or even *see* it as an interval. We see it as a personal failure. I found that I went by these intervals quickly when I recognized them for what they were. In the Enneagram, recognizing them would be the knowledge of the preceding lower *and* the succeeding higher: one will always be taken by the preceding lower; the attraction of this preceding lower is the only influence on me, but when one recognizes and accepts the true situation, one can become receptive to a succeeding higher vibration.

Intervals have a very unique taste and give very unique impressions. The acceptance of this idea is not easy for us. One reason for this is that we live in a dream. We repeat and repeat many times unnecessarily, but if we just keep repeating mechanically, we'll need a thousand years to evolve. We don't have that kind of time. We need shortcuts and the knowledge we get by struggling to develop understanding and being. It takes intentional suffering. You need to learn the *taste* of *Do*. In the Enneagram, *Do* is either active personality or passive personality. *Re* is the methods of the work. *Mi* is the reconciling force. In the Enneagram, bringing the law of three and the law of seven together brings a new way of understanding, which is very practical.

7.05 Q: You often speak about change of state versus change of being. Can you expand on that idea?

JB: I developed two primary Enneagrams. The first is the Enneagram of the Change of State and the second is the Enneagram of the Level of Being. The Enneagram of Change of State deals with short-term changes, something that could take place in a moment, in an hour, or in a day. One will then go back to what could be called the center of gravity of one's normal state. Everybody has a certain level of being, or central hydrogen. Your level of being is determined by your central hydrogen. Let's say my level of being is H192, but to evolve to H96 it moves through 191, 190, 189, 188, right on up. There are no jumps, and every movement is earned. The Enneagram of Change of Being takes place over years, a decade, or a lifetime. These two Enneagrams may have the same notations at the same points in the hydrogens, but in change of state one can move through an influence, through struggle, through meditation, through the impacts of life, a very strong shock, or a teacher, or doing Movements. We've all experienced a change of state. You can move through this Enneagram quickly, but you will always come back to your basic central hydrogen, your level of being. To change your level of state is possible with struggle, with effort, with the methods that Gurdjieff brought us. To change your level of being takes *consistent* work over many, many years.

The question whether enlightenment is instant or gradual has existed for 1,200 years. In Buddhism I think instant enlightenment is change of state and gradual enlightenment is change of being. In intensive work periods, a much finer energy can be generated and change of state can occur. Or people will sit at the feet of a master who generates a much finer vibration; when people take this in, their state changes. Under new values of this finer vibration, money, ego, power, sex mean nothing! All one wants to do is be in the presence of that finer vibration, but the moment you move away from that influence, you put back on your postures, your tensions, your anxieties, your worries, your future, your past, and your dreams! For a while you were free, but then you find yourself back in your usual state.

Gurdjieff's teaching was not about change of state, but achieving change of being. One of the dangers in the Work is that people confuse them and have little knowledge or understanding of being. In their confusion, some people aspire to change of state. People come to live for that! It feels good. Some people come to their group meeting for their weekly energy injection, so their state changes and they are calmed. Gurdjieff says at one point that "self-calming is man's greatest sin; self-calming is the Devil." Certainly, change of state is important because it brings in higher hydrogens, but our *real* Work is change of being. An example I've given many times about change of being: As people walk down the road of life they come to a large stone, pick it up, and put it on their shoulder. Then they come to a bag of garbage and clutch it under an arm, until there's this huge pile of stuff walking through life. That's us, and we don't even know if we're still there, underneath. We've got to get rid of this baggage, this garbage we've collected throughout our life. Self-observation brings a light to see that all of these things we are carrying are unnecessary, and as you let them go, your level of being rises. At least, that's part of it. If over a period of time, through change of state, you get more of the higher hydrogens than lower hydrogens, your level of being *must* rise. This is a law; not even God could change that! But if you burn up those higher hydrogens through negativity, sleep, identification, and as life in general eats away at you, your level of being will be lower. It used to be that the road of life was so bumpy that in order to survive, you had to develop being. One would develop being just from the shocks. The bumps in the road would bring you to moments of consciousness and bring you higher hydrogens just to deal with it. Today, that road is too smooth. Today, even older people have no being. This is why people in today's world will desert their grandparents in a hospital or nursing home!

Recently I was struck by *the Gospel according to St. Thomas.* I think the third saying of Christ and I'm paraphrasing: If those that guide your being tell you the Kingdom is in the sky, the birds will precede you. If those who guide your being tell you the Kingdom is the sea, the fish will precede you. The Kingdom of Heaven is within you and without you, and unless you know yourself, you are in poverty. The key there is "*unless* you know yourself." "Know thyself" has come down through the ages. It's through self-knowledge and self-remembering that we start to achieve change of being.

We are in a Work that's based on change of being, and that is different work than change of state. Change of state is very important for change of being; that's the way one receives the higher hydrogens. But if you become identified with change of state, your level of being won't change. This is a trap for many people, even people in the Work.

7.06 Q: What is a super-effort?

JB: A super-effort is not necessarily a bigger effort but what Gurdjieff describes as an *unnecessary* effort. He said, "Only super-efforts count." You don't make a super-effort at just any time. He also says, "Every effort counts, no effort is ever wasted!" It seems like a contradiction, but it's not, because all efforts *are* necessary.

You first have to make efforts in the first and second triads of the Enneagram. These efforts are vital to the process. In the first triad the effort is *interference* with the mechanicality of personality; the effort is very much like putting a stick into the spokes of a spinning wheel. Your struggle is to interfere again and again. The first triad is a bridge to the second triad. The second triad is participation. You have to develop a place in yourself that can participate with the impressions you receive from the roots of your personality.

Participation is what people sometimes call the "effortless effort," meaning to remember yourself in front of an impression. The

95

effort is *centering*: it is not *doing*; it is *opening*, which is a different movement. That movement could bring you to the third triad where a super-effort could be made.

In my Enneagram, super-efforts are the way to actualize the third triad, which brings you to a reconciled note, *La* H24. (See fig. 5 in Chapter 13.) Every octave is like a ladder with its own value system, and every note is like a rung of the ladder. Every note has its own value system, its own morality, its own tempo or consciousness. And all the rungs of that ladder, the whole Enneagram, are all linked to the next octave by the third triad. Just as every note, every rung of the ladder is an Enneagram in itself; the whole Enneagram is a note in a larger octave.

One of the characteristics of the third triad is that one has to become receptive to the values of the next higher octave or Enneagram by making a commitment to those values. In the first triad there is no super-effort, there is only the effort of interference with personality. What happens when you say, "I am going to walk an unnecessary mile with no personality profit or even essence profit?" Everything in personality screams, "No, I'll get the paper while I am there," or "I'll do it later." In experimentation, you ask yourself, "What would serve the values of the next octave?" Think about this! If you were in the third triad you would walk the extra mile, not for interference with personality but for the values of the next octave or Enneagram to produce a change in your level of *being*. A super-effort is only possible when you struggle for change of being and stay in front of the *Si-Do* interval which connects to the next octave or Enneagram. For now you have to practice doing the unnecessary, like walking the extra mile in preparation for the third triad.

My personal experience with the third triad and a super-effort came when I first moved to Miami. Remember, I was diagnosed with MDS and very weak from it, and I was seventy-two years old. I would fly down to Miami, then drive three hours to the west coast of Florida, have dinner and meetings for two or three hours, then drive three hours back to Miami; that for me, at that time, was unnecessary! Because of the level of struggle of this effort, this work had a tremendous effect on me. I interfered with my personality to serve a higher force. It was in response to people whom I never intended to have as a group but who asked so purely, and from such a right place, "Please help us; please work with us." I couldn't refuse. I was called to higher values and could not refuse; and everything in me went to those meetings to serve that; the values of another octave produced a certain vibration that called and was answered. Because of the unusual and fortuitous way in which Marshall May was brought into the group, I really believe that higher forces were at work. I had known him since the late 1950s as a responsible in the Benson Groups and worked with him at Mendham, Armonk, and the Foundation. I knew he knew and loved the Work, and suddenly here he was living just on the cusp of Alligator Alley, the road to the west coast of Florida. We would share the driving. Because of my health, if that call from the people on the West Coast was answered only by me, I would not have been able to maintain it on the same level for a long period. There will always be forces for and against. If you can start to vibrate at a higher frequency, it causes the negative forces to be stronger, but you also awaken the angels, the forces that are *for evolution*! There is always a struggle between those two worlds. But when you are mechanical *you* are not participating in that struggle: you are under the law of accident.

The west coast Florida group is now an important group. There are wonderful people in it, they are a strong group, and they are coming to our work periods. You never know who among them might play an important role in the future of the Work; so one has to serve that. I don't know if this fully answers you, but the second shock is about transformation of energy. A super-effort could be the same effort as what you do in other triads, but it can only be made at the right place with the right energy. One of the main characteristics of a super-effort is that it would *seem unnecessary* to this particular level, but to the next level it *is* necessary. Maybe we all need to ask the question, "What is an 'unnecessary effort' for me, now?"

7.07 Q: How does self-remembering help us to receive impressions?

JB: Self-remembering is the separation of the sense of I from the mind, body, and emotions to a place that the centers can't go. That separation is what can open to an impression so the impression doesn't fall directly on the centers

A cartoon from *The New Yorker* depicted a middle-aged couple watching television, the woman saying, "I remember opening the can, and remember washing the pot, but I don't remember eating the chili." It is a true observation, because nature puts us a little deeper asleep when we eat; eating is closer to essence, and personality is afraid of essence. Whenever you get closer to essence—during eating, going to the bathroom, or sex—personality supports going into a deeper state of identification. It's possible for an impression to come through and give you a little bit of energy, but personality takes *that* energy and makes you a little more emotional. In a restaurant where the taste of the food forces itself upon you, everybody is talking. I have my babble meter wherever I go to a restaurant; if the babble is loud, I know the food is going to be tasty.

I can't begin with self-remembering, but I can go to a specific sensation of a part of my body and I can take in a partial impression. As I begin this struggle, I see my personality and I can make an effort to open to both sensation and personality simultaneously. This is a big struggle and it takes a long time because my attention jumps back and forth. I am so addicted to and satisfied with being in one energy instead of a triad of energies. Also, I am never in the same state for long. Christopher Fremantle once said, "The great knowledge is in knowing how one moves between states."

The effort to open to two forces intentionally is the same on every level. Each energy has its own circulation: H192, personality, is circulating in the social environment of your life; impressions related to H96, essence, are associated with the level of Earth; for Man No. 4, impressions may be on the level of the sun or the solar system, or they could be galactic. Energies that are more universal vibrate with an energy that has a larger circulation. All these energies have their own circulation; as you climb the rungs of the ladder of consciousness you deal with different energies.

7.08 Q: Gurdjieff speaks about three being foods: physical food, air, and impressions. It seems that the first conscious shock feeds essence and that the second conscious shock feeds something higher.

JB: There is a process to the Gurdjieff Work. First conscious shock, impressions as a food, all demand the division of attention. It demands self-remembering in front of an impression; self-remembering brings an I-am-ness which is not part of my mechanicality. Gurdjieff says there is a second conscious shock as well, which crystallizes the higher vibrations into a higher body. The world knows about the second conscious shock but has lost the knowledge of the first conscious shock. Our coarser materials have no possibility of transformation.

I believe *commitment* to higher values is the second conscious shock. People may commit to be Trappist monks, take vows of silence, or obey the orders of a monastery to reach that goal, but when people go to church or temple only once a week, the commitment isn't great enough to create a sufficient shock. Since they don't remember themselves as a practice, what appears as commitment is often for personality profit or essence profit. They may be called to a higher set of values but they don't know it's coming from their personality, not from a real wish for consciousness. They're thinking: "I love God. I am going to heaven because I am a good person." What a wonderful idea, but it's a fantasy It could be a commitment to the energy of H384 or H192, the illusion of security. Even if someone commits for the right reason, is it for the crystallization into a higher body? It could be they commit, but maybe they do it to interfere with personality and are not at the right rate of vibration for energies that *could be* transformed or crystallized into a higher body. The second conscious shock and transmutation become possible only after long practice on the first conscious shock, which consists in self-remembering and in observing the impressions received. *Right development* on the Fourth Way must begin with the first conscious shock and then pass on to the second shock.

The reason personality grows and essence doesn't is because personality uses the energy of essence. The vibration that essence needs is not generated mechanically. Through experiences in the Work, one becomes aware of the value of impressions, that they *are* food and bring energy. You take in something and excrete something after you take the nutrition out. Gurdjieff says, "We take in impressions and we excrete behavior," and we don't think about the gap in between. The great advances in science and the arts came from the transmutation of all the foods into higher vibrations. Think of Einstein, Bach, Da Vinci, and others; if those geniuses didn't eat food and breathe air and receive impressions, there would be no theory of relativity, no B Minor Mass, no Mona Lisa.

First conscious shock is *self-remembering in front of an impression*. What makes it the first conscious shock is the division of the attention to include both active and passive forces in front of an impression. When you live a more essential life, like a native in the jungle, it demands a more harmonious relationship between all three centers. When you are young you have moments, not many, but some, when you see and feel one with God or at one with the universe. Self-remembering is a very high, galactic energy like the real energy of the mind.

7.09 Q: Conscious labor and intentional suffering: What is meant by that in practical terms?

JB: Gurdjieff calls conscious labor and intentional suffering "being-partkdolg-duty" in *Beelzebub*. It applies on every level of the Work. You are really asking: What makes it conscious? What makes it intentional? I believe it is the demand to awaken to an attention that can be brought out of the path of least resistance. Conscious attention comes from a very high place. Just as there are sounds that I can't hear and colors that I cannot see, there is a consciousness, or vibration of attention, that I can't perceive in my normal state; but its characteristics can exist. One of its characteristics is that it demands being directed and divided. This struggle for consciousness, this work, is going against the ray of creation. Habitually, we live in one center at a time, as if under one force. The process begins by the effort to open to two forces simultaneously where I am two-centered for a moment. This creates suffering because I see active personality; I need to suffer that. And also there's joy underneath intentional suffering because I have received something, knowledge, an impression, a special high hydrogen. Gurdjieff said, "Faith, love, and hope are not possible for man anymore as he is (as

100

mechanical man). His only hope is the arising of conscience." Objective suffering is not on the level of emotions that we know. We can understand that, but we still don't understand what the vibration of real conscience is without experiencing it.

We don't realize how intelligent the body is or how intelligent the emotions are. We think in whatever language we are raised in which is by nature formatory. We don't realize that our centers are trying to communicate with us but they have their own language. There is something objective in us but we need to learn how to listen and serve! Connection with the real energy of the mind results in an intelligent state in which I can receive information through all of my centers.

7.10 Q: What is "the disease tomorrow" and how can one be cured of it?

JB: We see a piece of paper on the floor and say "I'll pick it up later," or "I'll do that tomorrow," when it's emotionally right or when it's mentally right, *but just not now.* Like considering, the disease tomorrow[1] is not an action; it's more like a very deep state of identification. In certain centers I may do things in a timely manner, but for another center, only when it is convenient. Active personality lives in a state of considering: it's *made of* considering. Part of its make-up is also this disease tomorrow, so whenever I can work on considering I'm working on the disease tomorrow. You must awaken. And when you awaken, how to stay awake becomes important.

The disease tomorrow
is no longer covered
by my H M O.

It is important not to allow active personality to imitate this new awakening; instead, you try to maintain the state until you reach the next station, which is essence. The ideas of identification—lying, stupid sincerity, and clever sincerity—all demand a work that cannot be done by active personality, or in sleep.

During a work project the disease tomorrow was the subject of a haiku.

7.11 Q: "Blessed is he that hath a soul, blessed also is he that hath none, but grief and sorrow are the lot of him who hath in himself only its conception." We've also heard that expressed as the situation of "being in between two stools." Can you share with us your understanding of the nature of such a situation?

JB: You could almost say blessed is he who is falling down the mountain, there is no effort there; blessed is he who is on top of the mountain, but woe to him who has to climb the mountain. To climb the mountain is difficult: there may be traps; you may have to fall down many times. Or you could say that, according to Gurdjieff, in the involutionary octave, sleeping man is necessary because he is serving a function in feeding the moon. One stool serves the involutionary octave, while the other stool serves the evolutionary octave, consciousness. Both are blessed in that way. They serve a function. In between the stools is the tricky part. There is pain in birth.

If you realize that we're not born with a soul, as Gurdjieff says, but have a possibility of developing a soul, you move into a different arena than people who believe in heaven and hell. They may be asleep, but for them there isn't this underlying trepidation about where I am or what's at stake. If I believe I have a soul and will go to heaven automatically, I won't understand that what's at stake is a very, very big thing. If you believe in an automatic heaven and hell, there is nothing I can teach you.

There is a magnetic center that seems to be implanted in very few people in the world. What is a magnetic center? It is something in us that's not easily satisfied, impelled to find a way to objective consciousness. If one's magnetic center is weak, it could be satisfied with false ways and false gurus. But if it is very strong, those people will go past all the false ways and false gurus. Out of millions of people, only a few feel the need for objective spiritual growth. Some echo of it must be present in almost everybody, because religion is based on it. People are called to what Christ calls "awakening and being reborn." People are touched deeply, so there must be something.

Every false guru has a whole number of false disciples. But for a real guru there are only a few real disciples. Christ had only twelve. Gurdjieff carried on the Work with only a handful, not different from Buddha or others. I believe the people in the Work are the courageous heroes of our day. There are not many.

When you begin your struggle for consciousness you have to get off the first stool and step into your helplessness; if you work, you see you are asleep all the time, but you are no longer comfortable with sleep. You start to receive impressions of yourself. When you open to certain features they fight back and intervals come. It's a struggle. But at least you know the consciousness of it. We say "Woe to him who is between two stools," but at the same time there is greater joy for those people who are between two stools because they start to receive real impressions for the first time. People reach an interval and then they lose it. It is not permanent yet. There are joys, heartbreaks, and torments on every level.

Mechanical suffering is the pouring out of the vibrations you're in; you're losing the stuff of your life. Then there is a different kind of suffering, what Gurdjieff calls "intentional suffering." The bringing in of a higher vibration and that also comes with joy and a materiality. With intentional suffering you are potentially gaining change of being, not just change of state. When you are more unified you are at an intermediate stool, but then you have to sacrifice what you've achieved if you wish to receive the vibrations of the higher centers, a whole other world of the miraculous that comes from outside the solar system, a much greater circulation.

7.12 Q: What does it mean that we don't have a soul but only a possibility?

JB: The higher centers are brains in us which are able to receive vibrations that come from the galaxies. These vibrations are everywhere at once. The problem is that we are not receptive to them. These higher energies start to support the evolutionary path; they can start to coat in us a body that *can* be receptive to these higher vibrations. The intelligence of the higher centers knows everything about the higher bodies. But with an astral body, one can acquire an illusion of will, permanent I, and consciousness. In *Beelzebub*,

Gurdjieff says that "when a man dies, the astral or 'Kesdjan' body will start to gravitate towards the 'solar' body," which is the next highest being body. And for a period of time it may keep acquiring these higher vibrations. But if these higher vibrations are not acquired within a certain period, the astral body will disintegrate.

7.13 Q: Can you talk about your understanding of the four states of consciousness?

JB: People in the Work have all read about the four states of consciousness: sleep, waking state or waking sleep, self-remembering or self-consciousness, and objective consciousness. Physical sleep is what we do at night. And we live in waking state. Gurdjieff says we even know about objective consciousness. He said that people can experience objective consciousness; in states we can go anywhere but that you can't have objective consciousness in a consistent manner without achieving self-consciousness. And the reason we don't know about self-consciousness is because we think we already have it.

I believe the first octave in this band of waking sleep is the octave from H384 (false personality) to H192 (personality). Essence H96 is part of the higher octave of waking sleep. It's closer to self-consciousness, but you can be in essence and still be asleep. We need to experience states of essence and self-consciousness; as you receive more higher vibrations, you start to move upwards in this band.

As I started to work on myself I discovered that there is a certain distance I can go intentionally, consciously. I found that through struggling with my attention and working on myself in front of groups, I could move up just a certain distance. I had a certain range. When I was in a state of deep identification, lower in the band of waking sleep, I would move up closer to essence. If I began in a higher state, I would break into essence; or if I was in essence, I could even reach states of self-consciousness which helped me as a group leader. Then, there were times I didn't prepare properly and the taste of experiencing myself was so painful that even though my state would move higher, it wouldn't move high enough for me to be of service to the group. I would really taste the depth of my identification, and it was unbearable. Later, as I had more experience, on the day of a meeting I would connect with myself constantly because I couldn't bear the impression of how I would be if I *didn't* prepare. I knew I had to get higher in the band of waking state. As I became more essential in my preparation, I started to break through into self-consciousness more often.

There are two octaves in the band of self-consciousness. The lower octave is Man No. 4: You have some unity of the centers; you have astral matter in you, but you don't have an astral body yet; and your aim, as Gurdjieff describes it, your life, is for consciousness; everything serves consciousness. You must have already eliminated all the deeply identified sleeping I's and the remaining I's now have to serve the real Steward. Then there is Man No. 5, who has unity and permanent I, but is still in the second octave of self-consciousness. If your struggles have moved you to the left-hand side of the Enneagram, and if you are in that octave and become receptive, you can receive objective consciousness, the energy of the higher centers.

Think of states of consciousness as bands of two octaves rather than lines or thresholds, and that essence is also part of waking sleep. Men No. 4 and No. 5 are part of self-consciousness, and Men No. 6 and No. 7 are part of objective consciousness. At least, this is how I understand it.

I can't bring self-consciousness right away, but I can bring a representative that demands my awakening and self-consciousness. There is a representative on every rung of the ladder. This is what is meant by "God is good." He's given us a representative of the higher on every rung. Otherwise, how can we work, if we don't have a representative of a much higher rung that may not be available to us directly?

7.14 Q: What is will in man? Can will be acquired?

JB: The idea of personal will is an illusion. Every moment we are serving something, whatever center is the origin of what you are doing, whether emotional, mental or physical. Within the centers there are certain likes and dislikes, wishes and requirements. You are serving these.

There is a work in which you see what you are serving. Before you can serve something higher, you must work to see that you're serving something lower. In reality, it is a very big thing to see yourself serving something lower because we don't know that we are serving anything. We think we have will at our level: I do this, I do that. We think we are doing, which is will, but we're not. One can't do! Once a woman in my group said, "I can't believe we never do, because I 'do' all the time." I didn't argue with her. I said, "You have the right to your opinions." Six months later at a meeting she said, "You won't believe what happened. I had the task to be present at ten, eleven, and twelve. I was present at ten, and then suddenly at six in the evening I woke up and looked back and realized I didn't exist for the last eight hours. It wasn't that I was asleep, as we normally say; I was *nothing*." That is when I said, "Remember six months ago when we spoke about will and you said you could never believe that?"

It's truly a shocking experience—not just that I was asleep, but I was gone! What's even more painful is when you start to see you don't know what you were serving for the last twenty days *or the past ten years*. That is a shock, that's suffering, to realize you don't know. I believe Gurdjieff was very kind when he said we are asleep. We are actually in such a deep coma *there is no existence*. How could one do in nonexistence?

I'm bringing this as a preface to the idea of will. I don't even know which center I'm in or am serving. I'm often in the wrong center for what I'm trying to do. There is no choice if I am asleep. It's only when I awaken and see and accept the fact that I am serving something in my ego and personality or in my essence that something can rise that wishes to serve something higher.

Will is something that is of the universe, of God. God is very remote, way above the ladder, but He has representatives on every rung. What would it mean to be able to serve the next rung, in a practical way? Even though I may intend to serve, what does it mean *to be able* to serve? One has to first be receptive. It means to know what to serve or to be able to find the next higher frequency of vibration. Then, when you are able to be receptive, will becomes not just an idea but an energy. When *that* inhabits your body, you cannot help but serve. I sit here now and I wish to serve something higher!

106

What does that mean? I have to be aware of an energy in me. I don't have to think about what to say, how to formulate it, to make it sound good. All I have to do is have this energy in me that knows what to say and my mind will serve it. There is no momentum for consciousness. Each vibration has its own level of consciousness, its will or the representative of will, its tempo, its circulation, its location whether it's up in my head, in my feelings, or in the solar system, or the galaxy. So the moment I put it into words something is put into question and the attention is often taken by the path of least resistance.

What does it mean to remember oneself, to be present to allowing these vibrations to exist as vibrations, not through their characteristics alone or their manifestations, but just to *value the energy*? Let's say I'm in a state where I feel bliss and ecstasy. Bliss is the energy going through the emotional center, a way of releasing it. A characteristic of these higher energies is the feeling of joy and bliss. The vibration itself doesn't have bliss. Experiencing bliss is the beginning of a descending octave or triad. If I understand that, if I go with the middle, the bliss, it will be higher for a preceding lower; then I can even search for the finer energy again, and maybe in a new triad the succeeding higher could come. I need to search to maintain the inner vibration which is cooler, not necessarily emotional.

Can will be acquired? What *can* be acquired is the ability to be able to serve the next higher rung of the ladder. Again, if you can't be open to the right vibration, you can't serve. You could try, and in the attempt, there is value. One has to try and fail a thousand times. Drop by drop you develop the finer vibrations through struggle, and then, suddenly, the right vibration is there. It comes as a result. That's what Gurdjieff means when he says "No effort is ever wasted." If I struggle, I'm depositing something, but failure or success is not part of the equation. At first it is a struggle of putting a stick between the spokes of a spinning wheel, and later it's a struggle of letting go.

In a conference, Michel de Salzmann once said, "Gurdjieff was a slave of God; he served God." Someone asked, "Does that mean that we, trying to serve Gurdjieff's ideas, are slaves of Gurdjieff?" Michel said, "No, it means you are slaves of a slave." A little different connotation! Will is above. Even Gurdjieff was serving a higher will.

At one sitting Mme. de Salzmann said, "It's very important to be aware of the sensation of different *vibrations* in your body." The next stage is to trust these energies of my being, rather than impulses that are only reactions from external influences. One starts to trust these higher vibrations that are *not* conforming to outer influences of life; when I have the life in me that is not conforming to the outside influences and I *trust it*, my outer life conforms to it. All I have to do is wait in the right way and everything I need will come to me. This could be a reflection of conscious will; it reflects how will works. There is a conscious force that begins the process and everything is created for that. It's like the idea in nature that the flowers don't worry about the bees coming.

7.15 Q: What can I serve?

JB: The question is not "What *can* I serve?" You can't start off that way. The question that starts the process is "What am I serving?" Unless you know what you are serving, nothing is possible; even if you find you are serving something lower, this is a much bigger step than not knowing you are serving something. Only when you start to see you are serving something lower is there a call for and a need to serve something higher.

7.16 Q: Can you explain sensation more in depth? You've said that one has to understand the difference between sensation the verb, the action of trying to sense, and sensation as the object of such an action, the energy that is being sensed. Can you explain this distinction?

JB: In a sitting Mme. de Salzmann said, "One must be very sensitive to and aware of the different vibrations in us." At first we find just two or three. When you start to experience these energies you see the different "colorations" each one has and you understand that everything is under the law of three. By being aware of the right triadic energies, those that are triadically related, you may start to sense even finer energies. As you work in this way, you are working with different centers.

It is not just sensing the body and there is not just one vibration. It's a whole octave of vibrations. Like with pain: I can squeeze your finger or put it in a flame—a very big difference. If I sense my hand lightly and my attention is taken—I'm gone! I found that if I intensify sensation, not just exclaiming at the first touch, "Ah, sensation," but if I realize it is something that has to be maintained and deepened, it's possible to find a vibration that doesn't die so quickly. Just to *sense* doesn't really work, but by *deepening sensation*, even though my attention goes, the sensation doesn't and it calls me back very quickly. And I go back and forth and keep struggling.

When one has collected all the parts of their body with a collected attention, one could go further. There could be the resonance I spoke about, hydrogen 24. I'm opening to the resonance of the *whole*, but I open to it *through* a part. If I understand centering, it makes it easier because the centering is connected with the whole in a special way. Usually, a part immediately opens to the whole like a doorway.

What is the difference between the sensation of the flesh and the act of sensing? We must have respect for what it is that *senses*. The mind is not going to sense itself. It can't. But the body *can* sense the mind and bring about an opening to a new attention or consciousness. The language we use in the Work must be more exact, and it can only be more exact if we have experiences to draw from. You don't really know it until you experience it, and as Gurdjieff says, "Unless you relate the experience to the right idea, it will invariably be lost."

I remember leaving Mme. de Hartmann's house one day and walking to Central Park. Suddenly, I was filled with extraordinary love like a pulse flowing through my body, wonderful, as though I was plugged into an electric socket. It was an extraordinary vibration. And I realized that maybe this was the first time I felt that. It was not the usual loving someone or something; it was *a state of love*, which is very different. It still lives with me. This is not part of memory but a living moment, and it was fifty-three years ago. That's the kind of feeling we need when we are trying to create a higher body. That is the kind of vibration that the astral body can be made from; it can't be made of our emotional reactions or the contents of the centers. That's the natural energy of the emotional center. I've had a few moments in which I touched something like that, but it was always taken over by the emotions or the mind or body and put into content. The experience has to be guarded as precious.

Sensation is very important, as a verb; the act of being able to sense all these energies, the body, mind, and feelings and then being aware of the lack of connection with these energies as I usually am. Once you have had that experience, you can then know when it's not there. This is where the exercises of prayer that we talked about come in. You have to live with this and see. When you work no one can say what you will reach in that moment. The Enneagram shows it: in the Enneagram of Change of State you can reach the highest level at any moment; you can "become God" for a moment, but you always come back to the center of gravity of your level of being. We can never know what energies have been deposited already: like salt in water dissolves until it reaches the saturation point, and you never know when you'll reach the saturation point and crystallize the finer energies that would change your level of being forever. That's why we can't work for results; if we think "result," we'll never get it.

It's very important that you have an understanding of the ideas so that when you have an experience you make the connection to the right idea. That's one of the things a group leader does for a long time. Until you can do it yourself, they help attach people's experiences to the right ideas.

7.17 Q: We say that Work methods bring an active force into one's life. Is it also possible to begin with a passive force?

JB: I think the science and physics of today actually are having results that show the triadic world, but they don't know the law of Triamazikamno so they can't relate it rightly. Attraction may be the basis of many things, possibly even gravity. Gurdjieff brought the Work as a spiritual science based on fundamental laws. Many religions, which may have started out the way the Work did but have since *devolved*, may originally have begun with a passive force. Gurdjieff understood that we, as humans, can't start an evolutionary triad from the proper, passive force; because personality thinks of itself as the higher force, so we keep beginning an involutionary or descending triad and octave. Personality is *active* in us: it's not passive/receptive; it twists the will of God for its own benefit, the reflection of what Gurdjieff called the organ Kundabuffer. It was put in us to keep mankind asleep, but even after it was removed from humanity, its effects and personality being active has remained. I believe I'm awake; I believe I'm doing. This is active personality, and because it's in the dark, it's sometimes very bizarre. And it's all under the law of accident.

Gurdjieff understood we need to start with the active force. When you bring a task into your life it represents an active force. There are certain exercises that could change your state. But without tasks, there can be no change of being. This Work is about acquiring self-knowledge, the struggle between active *Do* and passive *Do* to attract the real consciousness that comes from above. Bringing a task for consciousness will create a struggle because what you meet is not passive *Do*, which would be part of an evolving triad. Instead, what takes place is an aberration. These two active forces repel each other: I want to do the task, and at the same time, there's great resistance. What is the resistance? Personality is active and it doesn't want to let go. There's a natural lawfulness in this tension, this repelling force between the two. I have to maintain the attention open to two forces which create the triad; this friction brings a "light" and results in seeing. Now I see this active *Do* for what it is: a bizarre trap. Active *Do* can't operate in the light; if it is seen for what it is, it dissolves, and passive *Do* is there instead. That begins the evolving triad, and here's where I need to understand, not only the tasks that wake me, but also tasks that I can then bring which will interfere with active *Do* imitating passive *Do*.

In this new triad, by maintaining these two forces with an active attention, passive *Do* and active *Re* can be reconciled at *Mi*, in essence, where the energies of three centers are moving by themselves. They're not unified, but they all exist: I'm three-centered. We're now talking about the first triad in the Enneagram. Working this way, over a period of time you start to eliminate a lot of the active I's of personality, and you start to have I's that can relate to what Gurdjieff calls "deputy steward."

111

If I struggle consistently, my personality is more friend than enemy. The evolving triad can be actualized so much more quickly. It's not so necessary to have this long struggle, in which you bring the active force to another active force; that's eliminated. When you begin with the passive force, you can then open to the direct energy of the active force. *Now* I do the task not to wake up, but to not fall back asleep. Beginning with passive/receptive force, when you're bringing in active *Re,* you're bringing a representative of self-remembering, such as a task, and that representative can have an action which can go on for a very long time, maybe years.

We can also start from the third force, the reconciled force; this is very advanced. In this particular triad I have to know my aim and keep my aim every moment so that no matter what I do it's in the direction of that aim. In life, I have a wish to do something, to be present, or to achieve something. Every moment I'm aware of that wish means I can't be identified with my turning thoughts. I still have turning thoughts, but I have to be at a level where I'm not a victim of associations, of my negative imagination or emotions or of postures and tensions. My aim has to be in all three centers. Something in me knows that's my aim no matter what I do. Gurdjieff asked someone after returning from being asked to do something, "How did you do it?" He said, "Very good." And Gurdjieff's answer was, "Very good is not good enough."

When we got our loft in Manhattan, which we had for eleven years, the asking price was way beyond our means. I went to lease negotiations with two of my older students and gave them the task, "Don't say a word, but every moment keep the recognition within you that we must have this loft." The loft owner said, "Well, we can't go below $3,000 a month." We said, "We will only pay $1,500." And these negotiations went on and we spoke of all sorts of things, and every moment we knew we had to have this loft that we needed this loft, and every word had an inflection of that. Then, as we sat there, quiet, he said, "Well, you know, I could let you have it for $2,500." And we continued to wait, and then he said, "$2,200." And then he said, "I can't go below $1,800, but I'll tell you what I'll do: I'll give you three months free rent." And that did it. It was amazing. We didn't have to do anything. We just sat there, the three of us, vibrating certainly, but with this one thought in mind: we must have this loft because it is the perfect place for us. Something changed this hard-bitten businessman. We watched him change in front of our eyes. That was the power of starting with the third force. But you have to be prepared. If you can't go against your associative processes, if you can't relax your body, if you're going to be in the future and the past, how can you work from the third force? If your personality's totally active and you're doing it from ego, how can you work from the passive force?

The exact method, the precision of the Work, is being lost by the way the Work is being brought in America. Subtle differences in how tasks are brought, when and under what conditions, turns them from being an active force to being worse than useless, even dangerous. They are nothing if they don't wake you up. Tasks have to be brought by a group leader who is a vessel for active *Re* 48 and should be in the octave of Man No. 4. If someone bringing a task is in the octave of Man No. 1, 2, or 3, they can only bring self-betterment, the idea of the Work, self-improvement, personality, a better life, which are side results of consciousness. If you are conscious, you will think better; but thinking better doesn't mean you're more conscious.

7.18 Q: What is initiation? What is meant by the idea that the only possible initiation is self-initiation?

JB: Initiation has a very important place in any work. We've spoken about interference, participation, and experimentation as an example. I need to start with interference, the first triad of the Enneagram. There are many octaves in interference. Let's take it from the point of view of our life, our being. You climb the staircase or the rungs of the ladder of the work of interference, struggling, developing an attention that can expand to include two forces; that work is the same for participation and experimentation too.

At first, your center of gravity is in personality. As you move closer to essence you can open the attention to the triad of participation. But you need to be initiated into participation. Where in the first triad, in interference, you're dealing with representatives of self-remembering, here in the second triad, participation, self-remembering ranges from dealing with the sensation of I to the feeling of I, dealing with a quieter mind. How do I do this? It requires something that can participate. In the first triad you're setting up a place that could later participate with your life, a new place in yourself that could be separate from the functions and will have an action of separating the contents of centers from their energy and unifying them. This work we call centering. Many people are not yet able to move from interference to participation. There's a lot of work that has to be done first.

As far as I know, with Gurdjieff's pupils, no one got this initiation unless he or she deserved it. Now people are receiving positions and "initiations" because they're relatives or friends or for some other reason. I observed that when people were given a role they didn't deserve it often turned out to be disastrous for the Work. You're not doing people a favor by bringing them into an initiation that's beyond them; you're doing everyone involved harm. A lot of people born into the Work, people who are favored, are being harmed because they haven't been prepared to move into places of responsibility. In my own groups people don't get a place unless they deserve it. And nobody can say how long an initiation may take. Everybody has his or her own rate of speed.

It saddens me to know that so few groups are working with tasks of interference, much less on participation, which involves centering. This work is being lost, even though Mme. de Salzmann stressed its importance. I fear for the future of the Work!

7.19 Q: Is there a work to do when I taste an interval? You're saying the shock will be provided, but how do I stay there as long as required?

JB: This is why one has to develop presence, the ability to be present. We don't live in the band of self-consciousness, we live in the band of waking state of consciousness.

If you know what I'm saying, there is a special taste to an interval; you will begin to look for it, instead of saying, "I'm in a bad state, and I need to get into a better state. What can I do? Let me call Jerry, let him fix me." I never work at that moment because I'm descending. I don't wish to taste my descent. It's an interval, and the descending movement is very distasteful. This self-pity and automatic negative imagination are natural results of the descent, the result of that particular note turning active.

Following the path of least resistance, I don't stay at the interval; I avoid the impression, and I go far away. But now I realize this *is* an interval and I must take it on the chin. Once I started to do that, I wasn't having that descent and I was suddenly past the interval. You have to try it to see it for yourself.

7.20 Q: Can you speak about time?

JB: Today's my birthday. I sat down when I was fourteen to think about what I wanted to be when I grew up, and when I got up, I was seventy-eight. We don't know time in reality. Time flows, and we're taken. We don't use time.

According to the Enneagram, there's a series of hydrogens that connect with the ray of creation, or what's called the *involutionary* movement. Each note relates to the notes above and below, and every note, every cosmos, has its own center of gravity, hydrogen, or frequency of vibration. According to how I see this Enneagram, hydrogen 6 is an energy that has a circulation through the entire universe, unlike H384 which has a circulation of just one little I in my head. Gurdjieff mentions in *In Search of the Miraculous* that "inner octaves are very important," and that's the last we ever hear of it. In the Enneagram, inner octaves are extremely important. One of the things about inner octaves, in relation to larger octaves, is that all of the characteristics of the notes and the frequencies of vibrations are the same. In the miniscule part of the universe we represent, we still have the whole range of hydrogens within us that the cosmos and the galaxies in the universe have; and these hydrogens produce the same actions in us, in miniature. The smallest inner octave has the same series of inner vibrations as the larger octaves. As above, so below, and every degree in between. *What is in the cosmos is in me.* This may explain a very mysterious statement in the Bible that we are made in the image of God.

The note itself determines where I am; the hydrogen determines the value system and the force acting through it; and whether it's active, passive, or reconciling determines the direction you're going, whether you're ascending or descending.

As I am now, I'm in a swirl of associations that have their own mechanical time, perhaps 192, perhaps 384 depending on how coarse they are. I'm pulled mechanically through my life. One of the tasks we have in group work is to walk through a doorway and stay present to the first five steps after the doorway and to be aware of the sensation of my feet. I see the change in my tempo, to make it a tempo that is for consciousness, not for personality profit or even essence profit, not in order to enjoy the day, *but for consciousness*. This produces results way out of proportion to the struggle I made. I'm now participating in my life rather than taken by it. That conscious movement comes from something higher in me.

What happens when I'm awake, when I'm present? Time expands. Our joke at the Brewster work periods is eighteen days, six nights because it feels that way. The days are much longer, rich in impressions. One is much more present.

There's no such thing as time because if there was such a thing as time, how could it vary? Why do I think I could change time? To change one thing, you must change everything. Whether that is *really* true or not, I can't say, but I have had that experience more than once in certain moments of Work. I believe time doesn't move; I move. I move through a tremendous tableau. Everything is laid out: the future, the past always exist, all at once, everywhere in the universe. Maybe a shock could bring me to another part of that tableau. Things move in and out, and sometimes it can change you. I saw that as the truth. This realization explained to me why there could be seers, someone who sees the future or the past. How else could someone see the past or the future if it didn't already exist? And I saw that my *fate* is determined according to the state that I'm in, according to what vibrations are in me; these will determine the movement through time. Again these are my own impressions, coming out of moments of consciousness and work, and a connection with this energy of H24 that I speak about. It's from when I was very close to this energy, and it existed in me vividly for enough time. What is time but an invention of man? According to the Enneagram, my movement through this tableau would be determined by which

116

note of the octave I'm in and what force is acting through that hydrogen.

I had moments where everything mechanical is sacrificed, and I could become one with the universe. It sounds like a trite phrase. I remember having it so deeply where I wasn't only one with the universe, I was also one with every person who worked on themselves, with every teacher throughout time. And this is what I felt: like time didn't exist at that moment; at that vibration we were above time. Otherwise, time cannot be overcome because there are billions of years, infinite time, space—all infinite, so nothing can have meaning unless you go into another level of vibration that maybe timeless, or there's another approach to time. What we call time is still theoretical. How we understand time is theoretical. I'm not sure it's what it appears to be. That's as far as I can take you here.

7.21 Q: In our inner work are we trying to free ourselves from the ray of creation?

JB: What I see in my life is that I have the ray of creation *in me*, in miniature. I believe that if there's a *descent*, the energies becoming coarser, there must be an *ascent* of the energies becoming finer, which is the evolutionary movement. That is what I call the harmonious circle. I know consciousness is needed. Mankind may have been brought here for a reason. We're not very old as a species, and we're very new to the Earth. Consciousness is a force in the universe, and we're probably not the only ones involved in the return of the energy. I think the Earth, the sun, the solar system, even the galaxies are sharing this struggle to bring the energy back to the Absolute.

I believe that the universe is an island of vibrations, everywhere the same mix. When you make a soup, and you put salt in, the salt is everywhere in the soup. The same with the universe: cosmic rays, radio waves, everywhere, right now! The idea is to be a receptor to the right triadic frequency. I believe our universe is self-contained, and no substance is lost; everything just changes form.

One of the questions I used to have about Gurdjieff's description of the ray of creation becoming more and more mechanical, under more and more laws, was why it is called the ray of creation. And what I came to is a very simple answer: because it is the creation of the material universe that basically started with the big bang. Slowly, particles came together to form galaxies, suns, planets, and moons. Everything becomes denser and denser, more mechanical and under more laws. Even suns become so dense that they become black holes. Many think that at the center of every galaxy is a black hole. It becomes so dense, the gravity so powerful, that even light can't escape. All descents begin with the higher, active force, which meets the lower and becomes the middle. What makes that so important here is that there's only one influence on the middle, which is the preceding lower; *the succeeding higher is not yet there.*

My struggles brought me to what I call the law of triadic attraction by seeing how different energies attract each other. In our Work a group leader needs to be connected with a finer, more conscious energy—not personality, not essence. As a group leader I need to struggle to come to a meeting in a state from the level of Man No. 4, which means I come for consciousness; that's the reason I'm here. If I can bring the energy of H24 strongly enough, I can open to the resonance of the whole, a more essential state. If, however, I come into the meeting and my H24 is not so strong, and your personality *is* very strong, I'm suddenly struggling to sense my right arm. I'm not in H24. I'm now in what I would call active *Re* H48. I'm sensing my right leg, my feet; it's now directed attention, not a divided attention. I'm reacting to the personalities of the group. I see in my life when I look at the evolutionary octave in me the lower blends with the higher to become the middle, and unless I bring awareness, consciousness, to that middle and resist the preceding lower, I will never have the opportunity to be touched by the succeeding higher. If I can do that, the succeeding higher comes and the movement evolves.

I feel the law of Triamazikamno is equal in the spiritual world to Einstein's $E=mc^2$ in the world of physics. I think the law of Triamazikamno and what I've dubbed the law of triadic attraction are what's keeping physicists from understanding what may be other aspects of string theories. This is my own thought. When scientists discover how the law of Triamazikamno works it will help them understand gravity. The attraction of the preceding lower is what causes all these large objects in the universe to attract other objects. Yet, by itself, gravity is a very weak force; if it wasn't we wouldn't be able to lift our foot off the ground or jump in the air, so gravity can't be that strong.

In particle physics, they've found that if you change the rotation of a molecule that's connected to another molecule, the second molecule will also immediately go in the other direction, even if it is on the other side of the universe. It would almost immediately change its spin. And I believe that to spin one way is an active force; to spin the other way is a passive force. In nature every force has a material aspect to it. Take a protein: if you "fold" it one way, it will have a certain action; "fold" it another way and it will have a different action. Nature is like that. In the beginning, they say, there was matter and antimatter. Fortunately, there was a little more matter than antimatter or there'd be no universe. Maybe in an alternate universe there *is* no universe as we know it because there's no matter. There's also the other end of the stick, which is the evolutionary octave.

7.22 Q: Can you speak a little about accumulators?

J.B.:   There are two accumulators in each center, and when you start to work with a center, you start to use up the energy in the first accumulator of that center. Then, let's say you have a cup of coffee or take a walk: a shock; and if it's the correct shock and the right intensity, you jump to the second accumulator, which is described in life as second wind. Usually what happens is that the second accumulator runs out of energy before the first accumulator has totally refilled, and if the attention jumps back and forth, the accumulators finally end up with almost no energy. It is then that you could connect to the larger, main accumulator, which can connect you with the highest energies. I would say that would be very dangerous to do unless you're ready for it, unless you know what you're doing. There are people who Work themselves to death, but that's not going to be our worry. It's not working hard or long enough.

Speaking practically, I start to use up the energy of the first accumulator, but instead of moving to the second accumulator, it jumps to the first accumulator of another center. *This is wrong work of centers.* I start to work on something intellectual and at a certain point run out of energy in that center. So where do I jump? I jump to an accumulator in the emotional center, and I'm suddenly emotional.

We all have something we take to. Someone could be a great photographer, but when they try another activity they can't do it; when their energy runs out they jump to another center. When I was very young I used to run track, and I loved the feeling of second wind. I would run until it felt my body was about to explode, and this new energy would appear. But I couldn't sweep the floor for five minutes without becoming emotional. This is often why people can't do anything well. There's a certain point where accumulators reach a little blip, a jump, like when a record or a DVD skips. If it jumps to another center, you can find yourself tense and emotional, and you can't continue. A close friend of mine, an intelligent guy, could never learn to drive because every time he decided to learn, he'd become impatient, negative, and it affected his whole life. Everybody has a point in their career, that if they had their accumulators working rightly and could jump to the second accumulator at the right point, it would be wonderful. Their careers would advance unimpeded.

When I started to become a framer I was only able to sand well for a very short time, not that I didn't continue to do it, but at a point I would go into my emotions and begin to do it poorly because the physical center is required there. During this time, experiences that I had at Mendham and Armonk and the inner Work that was given by Mme. de Salzmann and Mrs. Sutta and Mme. de Hartmann kicked in. I had many small seeings, and I struggled with how "Jerry" operated in the special circumstances at Mendham and Armonk and in Movements. It took me a number of experiences, of seeing parts of it, seeing things around it, and breaking through at times. There was one moment when I absolutely saw how that worked while it happened. I actually was separated from it. I watched it take place; I knew that it was the accumulator. It was all obvious to me. I saw that if that switch didn't take place, my whole life could have been different. It's one of the reasons why wrong work of centers comes into play. Because the minute the accumulator skips or jumps, I'm now in the wrong center, and that happens almost all the time. You have to stay in the right accumulator. You have to stay in the right center for the task at hand. It was at that moment of seeing the actual movement of my attention that I became free from the mechanical jumping from center to center. From then on, I had the possibility of doing things very well. My attention no longer jumped from center to center. I was able to stay; and then, when it went into the second accumulator, the energy would get finer and finer. I saw it was possible to become a master craftsman; from someone who wasn't even good with his hands, I became the one who had to do great gilded portraits frames that would now cost up to $50,000. If you go into the Metropolitan Museum, you can see those huge frames with carvings; I did those kinds of frames.

7.23 Q: What is the difference between sensing and feeling?

JB: When we first start working on ourselves we live without knowing what center we're in, whether we're sensing, feeling, or thinking. When we are asked to sense our leg, we often hear "I feel my leg." This is not accurate. We are not feeling it; we are sensing it. Gurdjieff brought a precise language, and it's based on the division of the intellectual, emotional, and physical brains; they each work with different energies and at different tempos. One has these habitual three-centered connections. We can start to see that even though all three are operating at once, there is one which is often dominant at the moment. The examples of this are when we get sentimental we cry, or we get angry and our body takes an aggressive posture. As you start to see the division of the centers, you see that sensation and feeling are completely different vibrations. Also, one is often in the mind and mistakes *it* for sensation or emotion.

The mind is usually in the future or the past, identified with associations and formatory thinking; we don't know the mind through its real energy. Why do we believe what we dream at night? All the scenarios in my dreams steal my sense of I-am-ness. I believe I'm awake and conscious. The same mind that believed I was an elephant tiptoeing through the forest now believes it's awake, aware! I can't trust that. It's the same with feeling. The emotions are usually in a state of reaction from thoughts about the past or the future. I certainly wouldn't trust my emotions as a sleeping being. The real energy of the mind is foreign to us, and the real energy of the emotional center, faith, love, and hope, is not possible for us now. Later, through the arising of conscience, we will find the real energy of the emotional center. Early in the work we are taught to use the sensation of the body as the objective center to keep us awake and more conscious. For the health of the organism, the instinctive center needs to be more protected by nature than the mind or the feelings. The triad which includes the instinctive, sexual, and moving centers is closer to the life of the whole body and is of a more objective quality without the same aims and identifications as the emotions and the mind. It does bring a light, a force of attention. It awakens me! I need to know sensation just for this reason. The energy of the body is usually in the present. All it wants to do is vibrate. Sensation is trustworthy; it's a good beginning. One has to remember oneself when one works. If one senses and tries exercises and tasks but loses the aspect of self-remembering, the struggle for consciousness becomes mechanical. If self-remembering, which is an I-am-ness, is there, there's a life in it—a force, a higher energy, a vibration. Usually, we can recognize when that sensation has become mechanical because the "light" goes out of it, but one can work for years with a low energy of vibration and with a vague sensation of the flesh, with the result that your work becomes mental.

There are different kinds of sensation. There is sensation of the flesh, the life of the body, sensation of the real energy of the mind, and sensation of feeling. How do I know my feeling if not by sensation? Each of these has a different coloration, or characteristic, like a triad in a chord. It could be *Do, Re, Mi* or *Do, Mi, Re* moving to different positions; like a musical composition, when put together they become harmonious. Most of the time we're a single note, and that's all we know. To experience sensation requires the ability to direct or divide or expand one's attention to include another note. That will bring a light that will verify a lot of Gurdjieff's ideas through experience.

We start with sensation because it is the most available, but eventually personality will co-opt sensation to bolster its own sense of existence! One must not confuse feeling for sensation, or sensation for feeling. What would it mean if I sense my right arm, and at the same time, feel my right leg? Now you are aware of the energy of the feeling center which is behind the breast bone, behind the reactions of the emotions. This is not emotion; it's feeling. One can eventually see that there are different energies that can be used for consciousness.

What would it mean to be able to sense and experience the energy of the feelings, and expand them into the whole body as if inhabiting a suit of clothes? That would take a practice. And perhaps at the beginning one can't expand this into the whole body. The same is true with the mind. What does it mean to have my mind expand so that it inhabits the whole body? There can never be unity if the energy of the mind is confined to the head, the energy of the emotions stays in the breast, and the energy of the body is not expanded into the whole.

Everything comes down to *the unification of the centers*. In order for there to be unification, two centers come together at first, but eventually all three centers must inhabit the whole of me together. One meets blockages that prevent unification of the centers. For instance, we see the turning thoughts, postures, and tensions most clearly when trying to sense the lower part of the body. The emotions are last because they are so volatile and we are too identified with them, but they're very useful in acting as third force, the reconciling force, the unifying force.

A monk was spending the night by a fire when a
beggar approached and asked if he could sit
by the fire until he got warm.
The monk not only agreed but invited him to spend
the night and gave him half his dinner as well.
The next morning, when the monk insisted that
the beggar eat the last remaining food, the beggar
transformed into the God Shiva and said,
"Since you were so kind to me
I will grant you one wish."
The monk asked, "Would you answer any
question?" "Anything you like," replied Shiva.
The monk said "How long it will take me to
achieve enlightenment?" Shiva pointed to a large
banyan tree and sadly said, "If each leaf on that tree
represented a lifetime, that's how long it will take you to
achieve enlightenment." Hearing that, the monk fell to
his knees and began to weep tears of joy, thanking Shiva
for giving him such wonderful news.
Shiva, astonished, said, "I don't understand.
Each time in the past that I had to answer that
question, the results were devastating, and the person
went away sad and extremely depressed.
Why are you so happy?"
The monk looked up at Shiva with a glowing face
and replied, "For such a precious thing—
such a short time."

"The sexual energy is very fine energy. It has its own circulation."

8

SEXUAL ENERGY

8.01 Q: Gurdjieff is quoted as saying, "In the power of sex over people are included many different possibilities. It includes the chief form of slavery and it is also the chief possibility of liberation." In another place, Gurdjieff says, "One must first eradicate the 'dogs' in the village of the sexual center." What does this mean, and how can sexual energy be used and transformed for the purpose of coating a higher body for a new inner birth?

JB: Nature's purpose in giving us this energy is for the propagation of the species. Nature doesn't leave that up to us. Propagation of the species is more important than the possibility of an evolutionary movement for mankind. We're very much slaves to sexual energy. One could imagine all kinds of things in relation to sexual energy. One has to be careful of how one understands some of the things that Gurdjieff says about sexual energy. It's a dangerous subject to talk about unless you have real knowledge of it. Current work groups must acknowledge this. The sexual center, like the other centers, has its own coloration, and a very fine and volatile energy. When it's strong, the mind, the body, and the emotions are at the service of it. In the groups we're trying to find a finer vibration that isn't a coloration of any center. It is not necessary to be conscious to propagate. However, if people are too neurotic or too unbalanced, or twisted, the sexual energy often causes unintended consequences.

Sexual energy is often used by the values and structures of personality, not what Gurdjieff referred to in the food diagram as *Si*

12. The problem is people have sex with the *contents* of the sexual center, dreaming they are conscious. It becomes great fantasy and hysteria. I believe it can create great damage to the centers, maybe even damaging them irreparably. The contents are using the energy for their own purposes under the illusion of consciousness. As you see in the Food Diagram the energy is generated by all three foods, air, food, and impressions, which should come together and generate the right hydrogen for the sexual center to work with. As opposed to any of the other centers, the sexual center is not restricted with regard to energies it uses. The transmutation of energy is restricted by the fact that after certain mechanical shocks it takes a *conscious* shock to transform them further. When the food is developed as shown in the Food Diagram, mechanically, it produces what personality needs to exist.

At H96 sexual energy is more essential, and at H48 it could be the sex of Man No. 4, more conscious sex. At H24 it would be very close to its real nature and would be very powerful, being one of the properties of Man No. 5. At H12, it would be the energy of real, pure sex. I believe that the astral body is made up by several energies, a triad. It's the transformation of the energy of *Mi* H12, but I believe that *Mi* H12 is also triadically related to the energy of H24 and H6. Gurdjieff said in relationship to the food diagram, *Mi* H12 is what could be transformed into a soul. Again, one must bring the Work into every area of life, even into sexual life. By being aware of yourself you start to see more and more how the sexual energy is manipulated by the personality. But the sex center very rarely works with its proper hydrogen. That's why, in a group, it's better to stay away from the subject. We have to become more conscious before we can start to understand how to use sexual energy for our inner work.

With reference to Gurdjieff's phrase "eradicating the 'dogs' in the village of the sexual center," one can say that the dogs are the contents of the center picked up in an accidental way. One must recognize that every center is corrupted, and the sexual center is no exception. We have no barriers to prevent these dogs from invading, roving around the villages, no fences. We are at their mercy, and everybody's village is subject to these dogs. A little bit of head knowledge is not sexual education. We get educated sexually through accident, on the streets. As to using sexual energy for the purpose of coating a higher body for new inner birth, if one starts to be more present and starts to observe, one starts to see these dogs. The difficulty with the sexual center is that the energy is finer and quicker than the energy we use for observation. For example, it's very difficult for someone to bring their attention to the sensation of their arm during the sexual act. How do we take the dogs and make them into willing servants?

To illustrate, I want to share a story. When I was a young blade, I met this girl; we had a few drinks and went back to her apartment. When she turned on the light, the floor was full of cockroaches! But the instant the light went on the cockroaches disappeared! The reason cockroaches have been able to survive so well is that most are allergic to light. Cockroaches not allergic to light have been stepped on and squashed, but the German cockroach gets along very well with man because it is allergic to light. All those active 'I's' in my personality are like those cockroaches: they are allergic to light; they flee in the presence of this new resonance which took years to connect with, and I spent an equal amount of time developing a stronger attention before it started to assist in my life. The chief difficulty is bringing centering into life! If you really take a part of your body, intensify the sensation, and stay with it, it will relax that part and the sensation will get stronger and stronger. If it gets strong enough, you'll see that when you lose your attention, the sensation will bring it back. You're able to maintain consciousness and a presence longer. At times somebody would do something to bring out a feature of mine, and there would be an I without its protective mindset, without its protective postures and tensions. I not only saw it, I also saw where it had begun in me, and now its dominance was gone forever! I started to understand this nontriadic relationship of energy was like a disintegrating ray, and I realized this was an accelerated way not only of observation but of change.

I started to wonder how long this strong connection could last in the sexual arena. What I saw was amazing. It didn't involve what I did; it involved identification. What started out in my being identified with a certain sex act became a feeling of who I was with, and the two of us became one. I started to understand a woman's body, what it wanted, what it needed. Instead of me having sex only for my gratification, we started to have sex for our gratification. As my identification with these acts was eliminated they became useful to my work. I also understood that even orgasm had baggage and how to deal with that. The sexual energy started to be incorporated in my essence, and as I became more essential my mind started to clear. I was able to free myself in all the centers.

I discovered that I had a stronger sexual circulation. Identification limits the circulation of sexual energy. Sexual energy doesn't go through your whole body; it has its erogenous zones. I found that the sexual energy within the erogenous zones was circulating much more strongly, with a finer vibration which brought me a joy. But later it reached the point where this blend of energies started to become difficult to access. They didn't stand out as much. I couldn't isolate it as much. I couldn't use it as much. I thought that maybe it got weaker, or maybe I used some up. I explained it to Mme. de Salzmann. She said, "Yes, you have a problem. The energy is not vivified enough." Gurdjieff speaks often in *Beelzebub* about vivifying the energies. To move to the next stage this energy needed to be more vivified. What I needed to see was more subtle and at a deeper level

As sexual energy started to circulate in every cell in my body it vivified my experience because the sexual energy can contain a much finer nature, able to go through the whole body, not just the erogenous zones. It vivified this resonance; I could really bring it into life. You find that it's not the act that determines the sexual energy; it's the sexual energy that determines the act! The energy is unified in a way that helps both participants. Gurdjieff also said, "Celibacy is important for some people at certain times, or lots of sex at certain times, or a mixture of both." For me, sexual energy did not diminish; I could have sex or not have sex. But with this resonance, what we call hydrogen 24, I received such strong impressions, it refined the sexual energy. Sex became very important at that time to vivify the energy. In French they refer to the orgasm as "the little death," especially for women. How can one be totally receptive, to allow a wave of energy to cleanse the body? What we speak of now is how sexual energy can vivify the energy that is needed to cleanse the centers, to get rid of the contents, and allow the centers to work with their vibration of the rightful energy. Many people tense when experiencing orgasm rather than surrendering to the experience. This can cause harm. I believe the way men have their orgasms affects the prostate. Enlarged or cancerous prostate may be the result of not having a full orgasm in older men. My personal experience verified this. I had an enlarged prostate, but it disappeared when this resonance and frequency of vibration dramatically changed my orgasm and cleansed my body. This I refer to as a surrender.

"The Yezidi circle is not a real wall. As long as it's invisible it's worse than a real wall because a real wall you can dig under, or climb over, or knock a hole in it; but this wall is impassible because it's imaginary. Open one's eyes and I see it's just a drawn circle."

9

FAMILY AND INNNER WORK

9.01 Q: How can I work with my family—particularly, with my parents?

JB: At one time I asked Mme. de Hartmann about a task for when I saw my mother. She said, "When you're with your mother, really see her face, see her body; see her, take her in, not just through the mind." And I remember I tried to visit my mother, saying, "Oh, I'm not going to react." And she would say something and suddenly I would get irritated; she would get irritated; she would respond; emotional buttons were pressed, and we went through our habitual dance. But one day I really saw her. And the first impression I had was that she was a victim. How could I react? She had no choice, a victim of a life, of hereditary factors. At that moment I felt such love for her. The effect of that experience lasted for weeks.

That is really the defining moment of my relationship with my mother, and it brought tremendous feeling. When she died the impression was just dreadful. One has a tendency to edit. She was in a coma. Her eyes were actually taped down because they were just open. She was brain-dead. But I was then and am now so thankful that I had that moment with my mother. With family there's a strong essence connection that causes you to be more identified because personality is threatened. When I'm closer to essence I see personality is such a lie. Essence could exist at the moment of receiving

132

impressions, could grow with it; and this is what personality is afraid of and does everything to make sure doesn't happen. Personality feeds on essence to give it a body. When we try to be connected with essence, our personality will put up a wall. It will try to stop us from experiencing this. We're starved for real feeling or a closer connection with our essence. When you are more connected, you can take in the impression of family members.

That same experience I described with my mother I've had with strangers, an intensity of compassion and love. I also noticed that whenever I was closer to something a little more essential, like eating, going to the bathroom, or during sex, I would be in a deeper state of identification. There are certain times where you're given work with people you love, an important work. People don't realize how important it is to make that effort because we have a much stronger opening to our feelings, to our essence if we're present. But there has to be a preparation first.

We're given a certain amount of experiences like that. Gurdjieff says, "It's like fishing in a river, and at the end of your life you have what you caught, and you will not have more than what you caught; you will have some big ones, small ones, medium-sized ones, and that's your currency." That's what you're going to use to buy your passage to where you're going. In order to have fish, you have to go fishing. There is an analogy in an old cartoon: A man sitting with his fishing line in a pail of water, but there are no fish in the pail. So you have to first make sure you have the line, make sure you're by the ocean or by the lake. Then you have to make sure your hook is baited. What Gurdjieff brought us is the science of how to be good fishermen, because at the end, what we catch determines what we are and where we're able to go. An old boot fished up from the bottom of the river is not going to get us very much. Having our hook and line in a pail of water is not going to get us any fish at all. This is where tasks and Work methods come in.

9.02 Q: Is there any Work on remorse of conscience with one's parents?

JB: Mme. de Hartmann had me sit every day for a period of time and try to remember the bad things I did to people, especially

133

my family, and especially my mother. She said, "Try to remember a time when you made your mother cry." That went right to my heart. The minute I tried that, I felt remorse like you couldn't believe because I did make my mother cry, and I remember those moments vividly; I might have been six or eight or twelve or twenty. And that went deep into my heart, and so to sit and try to bring that back starts to vivify remorse of conscience, not cheap remorse and not guilt. It is a practice to start to vivify the emotional center.

Later this work with remembering was very helpful when I started to have a connection with the body and mind, and I was able to bring the two together. But then I couldn't find emotion; I never could find the real emotion of faith, love, and hope intentionally; but from trying these exercises I could open to this kind of remorse, and that helped for a period of time. Later I needed that very much, and maybe still do. Think of things you did to people, and you start to see something that has an effect of a positive energy in you because real remorse is very uplifting. It gives you a finer vibration. It has energy, a life; your emotional center vibrates. The danger there is feeling guilty, or cheap remorse, but with struggle you start to separate the two.

9.03 Q: When I asked about inherited traits, what I had in mind was the Yezidi who couldn't escape from a circle. I just came back from visiting my sister and mother and I could see how much my sister is like my mother, even though she thinks she's very different. And I believe I have the same traits as well, that I can't escape that circle. How can that be useful to my Work?

JB: When you're born you have certain hereditary factors, environment, your family, and their influences. Then you grow a little older, and you have influences from school, friends, and acquaintances. You can't control these influences or even determine what all of them are. These influences are all under the law of accident. We're under influences of all kinds. Every vibration in the universe is here right now. We're in a soup. As above, so below: that's the law. When you meet the Work you can be under a different influence; you now can be in a different triad, a different octave. All of that environmental and hereditary material becomes grist for the mill. You need that material. But you need a magnetic center to come to the Work. Everybody has the burden of their personality and the influences that created it to carry through life, and some of that comes from our family. All of these habits are created in the dark. Our habitual nature is not guided by light and by intelligence. So, what is habit? It's repetition. You might be like your father, and you might be like your mother, and you might be like your brother, all according to the law of accident. It's material for you now. Where it came from is not important.

The "Caucasian chalk circle," as it's called in a play by Bertolt Brecht, or the circle that the Yezidis can't get out of, are part of much larger metaphors and have much more meaning than that. You can equate the circle with our prison, our mechanicality, our sleep. Each of us is bound by that circle, its illusion. The circle was real to the Yezidi. It was a psychological wall. We are all Yezidis, Devil worshippers. What do we worship? Money, power, sex, the illusion of life security? We're trapped in it. It's much bigger than just your family. Only something like the Work helps people who want to be free of these attachments. Gurdjieff says, "People are in prison, and they need the help of other people who have been in prison and escaped, in order to get out."

A master walked out of his meditation room and noticed that all of his main disciples were sitting around a table having a very animated discussion.

Later, he called one of them over and asked, "What were all of you discussing so passionately a short while ago?"

The disciple answered, "We were trying to decide if we had finally reached a level where the Devil had stopped chasing us."

"No, no," said the master, "you are not that advanced yet. You are still chasing him."

*"I'm always lopsided, always the wrong centers
acting and getting the wrong results:
This is what you have to see."*

10

CENTERS

10.01 Q: According to Mr. Gurdjieff, every person has a primary affinity towards one of the three centers. Can you explain this idea? What do you mean when you say that the centers are magnetized? How is magnetism of the centers related to the need for developing a real center of gravity?

JB: Gurdjieff brings the idea that each of us has an affinity towards one center. There's Man No. 1, Man No. 2, and Man No. 3. One man caught in a fire says, "We have to move now," as he starts to run (physical man). Another gets hysterical (emotional man); he could be a physicist of the highest intellectual order, yet he's emotional and he will make decisions from his emotions. And mental man says, "We have got to figure out a plan to get out of here!" In the moment it will be like that! One could have a great physical body and be very involved in sports and movement but caught up in the brain. So it's not which center is developed, it's which center you're most identified with. I believe that predisposition to be Man No. 1, 2, or 3 is in the essence. As we are now, one of the problems we face is that we don't live in all three centers at once. We live in one center at a time. The mind, body, and emotions are tied together accidently, but these configurations are based on chance, like the pull of the lever of a slot machine.

I try to bring my attention to sensation of a part of the body, but the next thing I know I'm thinking or I'm feeling or I'm in another part of the body. Right now, the magnetism of the contents of our centers calls our attention all the time. So I may become aware of the state of identification, but I'm not aware that it is magnetism; the more the imbalance between the centers, the stronger the magnetism, the deeper I am identified. Whichever I supports the magnetism draws the attention. We now only know our centers through their pouring out of energy.

The attention can drive a wedge between the contents of a center, which are magnetized, and the real energy of that particular center. One center starts to become free, and in that struggle we start to find this new attention, find the energy of the mind, and bring that to the postures and tensions of the body. It's this attention that actually frees me from the magnetism. I start to learn that there is an energy that circulates and vibrates in my essence. The energy has been there but has been blocked by this magnetism. Then, at a certain point, I have to open to another center. One by one I start to demagnetize and find the rightful energy of each center individually. We start by interfering with the habitual turning of the center. This is interference.

What Gurdjieff calls "chief feature" is not going to be seen by one center seeing another because it's in all centers. However, the heart of it may be in the center I'm most identified with while its roots are in all centers. At some point I see enough of active personality and I start to know the life of these centers, and I start to realize that is not enough. I must see the roots of everything. True observation is not one I seeing another I within the same center; it is one center seeing another center. First we have to demagnetize the centers, separating the contents from the energy and bringing them into balance.

The work called participation is possible after proper preparation. We can start to have control over an attention from a new center of gravity that could resist the path of least resistance, the preceding lower. It's development of a new center of gravity that's not magnetized, that's not of the mind, body, or feelings. We know from physics that in order to have gravity you must have mass, materiality. In this struggle we start to find that there's an attention that can exist without being constantly taken by one of the centers, an attention that has mass.

10.02 Q: How can one reach and use the real energy of the centers?

JB: We live like we are going into a dark basement with a flashlight, and we shine the light and see a chair, a sink, an old carriage. We came down looking for something, but we become identified with each thing we shine the light on. We become the carriage for a moment. We become the sink. We don't see the light; instead, we become the objects and their shadows. These are the contents of the centers, and they're meaningless and transitory. What happens to the shadows when the light moves on? It's the same with the postures and tensions of the body. What we've lost is the light. The light is energy, and apart from the contents, each of our centers has a light of its own and a frequency of vibration.

It's the contents of the centers that have the illusion; that's what personality really is, *the contents believing they are the energy, the light.* But personality reflects the energy of the centers like the moon reflects the sun. Our personality reflects the light of our essence. But that's in the ordinary world. Also in the ordinary world, in life, it's possible for injustice to take place or to get what you don't deserve. Anybody in the right place at the right time can hit the jackpot and win millions of dollars. There are many cases of people getting something that they didn't have to work for. In the spiritual world, however, *nothing is received unless it is paid for. You must pay for everything!* Sometimes you pay in advance, sometimes you pay during, and sometimes you pay later, but you must always be *ready* to pay. You must have the attitude of wishing to pay in advance. In the spiritual world everything is lawful. In the spiritual world there is no such thing as injustice. People say, "That's unjust. I want justice." Ask yourself, "Do I really want justice?" You know what you would get: the deepest bottom level of hell. We don't want justice. That's the last thing in the world that we would want, after what we have gotten away with. There could be a light in us that one day will be

140

permanent, that will never go out. This is what is at stake in this kind of Work.

The problem is that the contents can never be unified. The centers are stuck together. For example, I once had a thought, and that thought stuck to a certain posture, and they stuck to a certain emotion, and an I was born. If I take that posture, then I have that thought and that feeling. Or if I have that feeling, then I'll take that posture and have that thought. I have many little I's like that, with their postures, voices, ways of formatory thinking.

How can we appreciate the light of the body? The light is also material of a certain vibration. I develop an attention that I can move, divide, and expand when I start to work in a scientific and consistent way. *Developing that attention is more important than anything else because that will be the ultimate tool for whatever I wish to do.* We use the attention to separate from the postures and tensions of the body. The energy of the body is a place to start because it is more available. Its part of the instinctive center protected by nature and not diminished as quickly as is the energy of the mind and emotions. If the instinctive center goes, we die. The energy of the mind isn't as available. I'm much more identified with my emotions than my body. Emotions are very strong. It's the same thing with my mind. It's hard to sense the energy of the mind because I'm so involved with conceptualizations of myself, of the conceptual I's; I *become* these turning thoughts. But as I establish an awareness, an attentiveness to the energy of the body, I need to then open to the mind. The opening of the attention to include two forces exists on every level: first, between the content and the energies of the centers; and then, when I have that connection with the energy of the life of the body, I have to open up to the energy of the mind—and the mind has many energies. If the mind is quiet enough and the energy is receptive enough, there are moments when one is more unified and can touch energies of the mind that are extraordinary, that may even come from the higher intellectual center, H6.

Before we started tonight I was sitting here quiet and calm. We talked a little about politics and life and I saw that had an effect on me. But as I start opening to the energy more and more, I see there is a shift. I'm searching for it now and I see it's partial, not completely vibrant and whole, but it's moving. Even the vibration of my voice, one can sense that. As I sit here, aware of the vibration of the body, I also want to open to the vibration of my mind. How does one do that? I find it helpful to enter the head through the spot between the eyebrows. It seems to me that when I am connected to my body and I bring attention to that spot and sense, it can quiet the associations and formatory thoughts. I find that to be a doorway to the real mind. I see my mind quieting now, a different coloration than the vibration and frequency of the physical body. I can tell the energies apart. It's almost alien when I first begin this because I'm not used to the vibration of my mind. All of this comes into my inner vision, and instead of identifying and becoming the contents of the centers, I now can sense them both. This begins a very difficult work because the vibration of the body and mind repel each other and to go further requires a very developed attention.

The impression of not having my familiar thoughts and associations is like dying or losing my intelligence, and I can't bear that. I don't realize that this state of not knowing is an intelligent state because it is in the present. This is what I mean by finding the energy of the real mind and being unified with the real body. What would it mean now to open up to the feelings? The doorway to our real emotions is in our solar plexus. Usually, I stop at the breastbone, but can I go behind the breastbone and sense a different coloration?

Gurdjieff tells us that the mind works with hydrogen 48, the body with hydrogen 24, and the emotions with hydrogen 12: the real energies of the centers are a triad, H12, H24, and H48. If the three real energies can exist simultaneously, they will start through the law of triadic attraction to come together in unity.

10.03 Q: How can one see the wrong work of centers?

JB: I had experiences with this. Certain I's in the mind get glued to certain I's in the emotions, which get glued to certain postures, so that when you have a certain thought you'll take a certain posture and you'll have a certain feeling; and if you take that posture, you'll have that feeling and have that thought. The centers are glued together by what I call the law of accident. These *ruling* I's that we

142

have in us are so strong because we're one-centered most of the time, but they're three-centered. They're three-centered little gremlins! And they rule us! We don't realize that. One of the main reasons I *can't* change is that I want to change one center only; however, I've got two other centers pulling me back to imbalance. I'm a slave to the magnetism of that movement. This is why we're told "Don't try to change," but this doesn't mean we don't interfere in order to observe.

That is the doorway into our prison, but the doorway into the prison can also be the doorway out of the prison. It goes both ways. For example, I may think, "I don't want to be irritated with her." But when I'm with her I take a certain posture and I get irritated, and then I say certain things that get me the opposite of what I want. I have a certain reaction; then I need to know that reaction's posture and its mindset. Or if I see the mindset, I have to see the emotional reaction and the body. Otherwise, I'll never have a chance. If I interfere with one center, I can start to see the other two centers, and it's very important when I observe a certain state. One I seeing another I is not self-observation.

Once I went to see a group of prize-winning movie shorts, and one of the shorts was called *Bambi Meets Godzilla*. The scene opens with Bambi peacefully chewing a daisy, when suddenly there's a loud thump and the whole screen shakes. Bambi looks up, startled! But then everything is quiet and Bambi starts chewing on daisies again. Suddenly there's a bigger thump, and this time the screen shakes even more. Bambi is startled, looks up, and nothing happens; Bambi again goes back to chewing on the daisies. Suddenly a huge green leg comes down right on Bambi—flattens Bambi—and after the foot rises there's a huge footprint and a squashed Bambi. And it says across the screen "Bambi Meets Godzilla—The End."

I thought it was very clever, but in thinking and talking about this, I saw the idea that in my life, my sleep, my mechanicality is unbelievably powerful. Let's say somebody steps on my pet corn and I get enraged. I have no choice about this. It's amazing how enraged we can get, even with people we love—whatever the situation, whatever injustice! We are helpless slaves to our mechanicality.

Now if I say, "I don't want to be negative," I'm Bambi, right?

And that negative emotion is really Godzilla. I usually have *very little* chance, especially if justice is on my side, or if I think I'm right. With my reactions, out pours all the finest energy and poisons are created in me. The mechanical union of the centers is glued together by the law of accident; I realize that I'm Bambi, helpless, but I can change the arena away from the emotions with the help of the Work. I found it an effective struggle against emotional Godzilla to move to the arena of the body by changing my posture. It's also possible to change the arena to the mind, which is what Ouspensky did a lot. Trying to count, doing all kinds of mental exercises could work for a while; however, I found that wasn't so effective for me because my mind was too much at the service of my emotions.

With the knowledge of the Work you can struggle with the mechanical postures of your personality. It's not easy, but if you can really change your posture, you have a chance to struggle against your Godzilla in life. Again, the doorway into the prison could also be a very clever way out of the prison.

10.04 Q: How is the wrong work of centers related to the differentiation between the contents and the energies of the centers?

JB: Let's begin by identifying the difference between the centers' contents and the energies. The contents of the centers are acquired in life and glued together by the law of accident. At this moment, the energy is invisible in our state of sleep. We see the contents and we think the contents are what is alive, but they're not. The real thoughts, real associations, and emotions are all energies; our postures and tensions and contents of the centers are coarse vibrations, mechanical in a mechanical world. They feed off the real energy of the centers to *exist*. One can never come to real unity of the centers through the contents. I once told a story to one of my students. We are created as if we were a computer on an assembly line that falls on the floor. A person picks it up and accidently pushes all the wrong keys, and that's the program of my life.

True self-observation begins with one center seeing another center, which is why we have to divide or expand our attention, why we have to be able to bring our attention to the body. There's a series of tasks that deals with how to see and observe the *contents* of the centers; this is what Gurdjieff calls "self-observation." Even though Gurdjieff said one can begin from the mind or the feelings, for a long time the sensation of the body is more available than the energy of the mind or the real energy of the emotions.

When we start to bring in another center in this way, we get an evolving triad; then we start to see and identify the content: it stands out as being artificial; it stands out as being the pouring out of energy, very different from the real energy of the center which circulates and doesn't pour out unnecessarily. It is this separation which allows me to make the distinction.

In special kinds of sittings, there's Work in which this division can take place much more quickly, but unless you know *how* to see it, you'll never work that way; you won't understand what you're seeing. You won't put it in the right place and won't understand that one has to go further. You have to learn to come to the Work with the real energy of the centers first, bringing them into recognition of each other so that the real energies of three centers will relate triadically. The centers start out of tune, and I must be able to maintain my attention long enough so that they can begin to relate to each other. Right now, as a sleeping man, I'm one-centered. That's all "I" want to be. "I" want to be identified with the mechanical part of one center and go along the path of least resistance. The gravity of the involutionary octave is identification. That's the pull. Work is moving into the evolutionary octave, in which every step demands attention. Gurdjieff would say it demands being-partkdolg-duty, conscious labor, and intentional suffering.

The contents have stolen my sense of I. This is why, if I die when I'm just the content of the centers, it's the equivalent of having been given a light when I was born but becoming only the shadows. What happens to the shadows when the light moves on? If there is to be a continuation, it's going to be a continuation of the light.

10.05 Q: What is the role of higher experiences in the Work?

JB: Gurdjieff tells us that the higher centers are already developed. It's the lower centers that are out of relationship.

I had some very high experiences, even when I was young in the Work. But I've come to realize that one could have these experiences, and the rule of the law that I've come to is that no matter how high an experience you have, you always come back to the center of gravity of your level of being. I know people who have had very high experiences, but I thought their being was so low because they thought they were so high due to their experiences. Their past experiences justified everything, even the lowest things—lying, cheating.

I realized at one point that people can experience high energies by visiting a place that has a sacred vibration; one could be open to that. Especially in religion where people might see the Virgin Mary, I don't think they really see a woman who gave birth to Christ; rather, they feel an energy which brings them into the higher centers, but their ordinary mind can't understand that or accept it, so the ordinary mind creates an image it can deal with. Edgar Cayce used to say about his trance state that he would go into a white hall and see a man with a long grey beard who would hand him a stack of tablets to read. I don't really believe that a little old man was hanging out in a white hallway somewhere. I believe that's how Cayce's mind saw the vibration that came from the higher intellectual center, which I believe Cayce connected with, judging from the transcripts of what he said in these states.

People have these experiences from higher levels; the problem is they don't have a vessel that could hold them, so they come back to the center of gravity of their level of being, which is a mechanical machine. What happened to this high energy? It's gone. A man who has developed a vessel can develop a new center of gravity, so if enough finer matter is produced and there's a triadic relationship, some of it is transformed into the middle and deposited in this vessel. He has to think, "How can I deposit astral matter, now?" Man No. 4 has accumulated astral matter; he doesn't have an astral body yet; he is in transition. Man No. 5 has an astral body. Our work is more the daily grind, the drop-by-drop depositing of astral matter. We need to make efforts and not work for results. You could say it's for the unity of the centers, what Gurdjieff calls the "Kesdjan body," the astral body. It's the first higher body. If it's receptive, it's what the higher centers can be attracted to.

10.06 Q: Is one held back by the center in which he is least developed?

JB: One could say "held back," but I would rather say one needs work on the centers that are less developed. This is our condition; we need to work on that.

For me, I came to the Work very much in my head. When I was young in the Work and first going to Mendham I sometimes had to feed the animals. They had cows, sheep, and pigs. On a beautiful sunny day I would have to go into the barn with a bandana over my nose, take hundred-pound sacks of barley, wheat, salt, or whatever, and make this huge pyramid of grain. It could be twelve feet high, and we had to turn it over, not once but twice, so that it mixed, blended. I noticed I did everything with my right side, so I started to alternate; maybe I was given a task at that time of working with my left arm. At first I hated it, and then I started to get such pleasure out of the fact that I was doing it with the other side.

10.07 Q: In the first triad, do we always create interference in order to bring another center?

JB: Well, it's not quite bringing another center. It's using a different center. You'll still be one-centered, but you're using a center you're not used to using in that situation. You are starting to exercise that center. Now we're talking about developing the sides of ourselves that we haven't developed, and that our tendency is not to develop and to follow the path of least resistance. This is a rut and I don't open and use parts of me which eventually may get rusted. Or as Gurdjieff said, "Like a coach that was built to go over rough roads, and the greasing system was based on the shocks from these rough roads that would force the grease into all the parts of the coach." But we now only travel smooth roads, so many parts don't get the grease and get rusted and locked together. When struggling with a task that requires me to bring a center I normally don't use there's a chance for it to receive new impressions and begin this process of balancing. We must never forget that the Fourth Way is a way to balance the centers. Some centers, in order to balance, need interference to help development. Don't forget that the center I'm in all the time is the one that I'm most identified with. You may be asked to go against

147

associations or to count every time you see an association, all kinds of exercises. In that way, you're developing your mind. Or if you're developing your emotional center, see your mother's face when you made her cry; that's an exercise for emotion.

10.08 Q: Is everyone who is in the Work indeed a part of, or "on," the Fourth Way?

JB: I thought for a long time that I would never find a Way, that I was too much of a skeptic. I went through many philosophies and ideas and rejected all of them. The moment I would question something with "How do you know?" and someone said, "You must believe," I would get my hat and coat and leave. And yet when I came across the Work, when I read *In Search of the Miraculous*, immediately in my heart I knew this was for me. I had come across the most remarkable teaching I could have ever imagined. In my wildest dreams, I couldn't imagine that a teaching like this could exist here, for me. The idea of the Fourth Way itself is a revelation. It's a truth that somehow you knew had to exist but was never formulated, and then suddenly there it was, formulated and coming from a high place, a high consciousness. And people who had worked with Gurdjieff, they're extraordinary! I think many people feel the same way when they first discover the ideas—an impact, so one feels that everybody in the Work who has that magnetic center, who searched and found this teaching, is in the Fourth Way.

But as the years went on I started to realize that some people in the Work went into their own grooves. Certain people were equivalent to fakirs; they wanted to do physical things, and they thought they weren't working unless they were doing something physical. Somebody asked me to make up a joke on the spot because somebody else had, and I said "How many Gurdjieffians does it take to change a light bulb?" The answer: "Five: one to change the bulb and four to clean the apartment."

There are certain people who love the Work with all their *heart* but they often don't know anything about the Work. They don't know the ideas, and many times they don't even make physical efforts. They even cry at times when they speak, very emotional. They're the monks; they believe in the Work, and yet they don't know it. And then there are the people who count the number of angels on the head of a pin, where the whole Work is conceptual, ideas, and in a sense you can equate them with the yogis. There are also some people who are really only interested in the Movements; to them, the Movements are the Work.

And then you meet people like Michel de Salzmann, who I felt was like my older brother in the Work, and others. You felt they were real seekers of the truth. Their search was still alive. I had never heard anybody talk about it this way, but I remember working this out and thinking about it, and really feeling that there are many more people who are fakirs, monks, and yogis, and there are fewer who are searchers in the sense of the Fourth Way, and even fewer seekers of the truth.

"We don't stay present long enough to have a deep impression of ourselves, and it's lawful.
When you practice centering you need to practice it, not for a moment, but for an hour or more
—an effort of being with yourself, of participating for longer periods of time."

11

CENTERING

11.01 Q: According to Gurdjieff, each center has a moving, emotional, and intellectual part. How can one know the different aspects of each center?

JB: We do know the associative part of the centers; the moving part. Gurdjieff does say that "self-remembering is being in the intellectual part of all three centers simultaneously." How can you know that? We were taught that you can know each part of the center by the way the attention works there. For example, you may be reading a book, but you don't really know what you are reading. You realize you jumped five paragraphs and didn't quite know what it meant or you get only the gist of it. Many times, you read like that; for some books this is all the writing deserves. You get the gist of the book that way. In reality, many times we read very mechanically, without attention. There is another way of reading. For example, I like detective stories. I'm reading a very good mystery, I feel a feeling, but it's not from the emotional center; something in me is dying to know what happens next, and I can't stop turning the pages. That is the emotional part of the intellectual center. For the intellectual part of the center, read *Beelzebub*. Gurdjieff wrote a book that you can only read from the intellectual part of the intellectual center, with attention. Generally, you can read all the books on consciousness in the world but not be an iota more conscious. *Beelzebub* is an exception; you must really have an attention because of the way the sentences were constructed. In *Beelzebub* there is no mechanical rhythm. This is why many people who aren't in the Work love that book because you sit down, read it, and when you stand up you are in a different state. I have had that experience and have used the reading of *Beelzebub* to get out of bad emotional states. Using the intellectual part of each center demands an attention out of the path of least resistance.

When you play sports, you are often in the emotional part of the moving center and occasionally in the intellectual part, but that's rare. I think this is what is meant by being in the zone, when you can't miss: in certain physical states you can throw a ball into a spot the size of a dime while running at full speed. When you walk you may be conscious, but you don't have to say, "I move my right leg or left leg." You allow the body to find a real momentum. We don't walk from momentum; we are so tense and out of balance with gravity, it takes energy and effort to walk. One could walk from an inner place where you can produce energy rather than pour it out or waste it. Gurdjieff describes it as "walking with the right kind of momentum." When one is in the state where the moving part is used in a right way - that is coming from the intellectual part of the moving center - which is the brilliance of work in Movements, and why people get so much from it. You can only do Movements from that place, the intellectual part, connected with the moving part, with reconciliation in the feelings. As a servant, the moving center is the holy denying, so to speak.

Emotionally, finding the intellectual part is where you have to struggle to have real remorse or develop conscience, where you bring a certain effort to get past your mechanical emotions, even past real feelings for some, or past falling in love or being infatuated or other things that touch you emotionally. The intellectual part of the center is another level, a feeling, not an emotion; it's the energy of the emotional center that is very different than this place we feel in our solar plexus. It's an opening to more parts of the body, a different energy. This is where I feel the energy of the centers comes into play rather than the content. The moving part of this center is *all* content. It is filled with it. We have the moving part in each center but they

152

are motivated and moving, not because they want to, but because the weight and impulse of the contents are causing them to spin.

The intellectual part of the intellectual center is the pure energy of the center and a different attention. Your associations don't move, *but they can bring you anything you want to know.* They are there, but they don't spin or turn. In this state I felt that the real associations, which we often despise and put down and think are in our way, are one of the greatest gifts God gave us.

There is an inner triad. Just as you combine and unify the three centers, you combine the frequency of vibration of H48 of the mind, H24 of the body, and the frequency of the emotion, H12, the pure energy of the center.

There's a task in the Work that when you wake up you put a book on your head and do the morning sitting. I remember vividly that when I did it originally I couldn't keep the book on my head for more than a few seconds. When you're present in your body you don't need to move from the moving part that has acquired postures, tensions, wrong alignment, or as Gurdjieff called it, lopsidedness; and then the intellectual part is something very different. Operating certain machines or doing very fine crafts demands that you do something from the intellectual part of the moving center. Or if you jump out of an airplane without a parachute, your friend jumps with an extra parachute, and you meet in midair: for a while your body is so attuned, I guarantee you there are no associations. Then there could come a time when it becomes mechanical, but for a while it certainly isn't. But this is a hell of a way to take in impressions.

11.02 Q: You mentioned something about the energy of the mind and associations. How does one connect to that?

JB: At one point, I discovered that associations may be one of the greatest gifts that we were given. But that's if they are the servant. When they're the master they *take* everything in you. It's a kind of not-knowing that's more intelligent than knowing. These associations that *served* and came out of quiet mind were extraordinary. I don't know what I would have done without them. The Enneagram came that way. I used to be in a state like that for hours, without any associations turning; and it was in that state that I wondered, "Why am I wasting it just like this? It's nice, I'm in a good state, but why don't I look at an idea of Gurdjieff's that I never understood, and try to understand it while I'm in this state of no-mind?" I realized I knew nothing about the Enneagram, not a clue. I never really understood it because the way I viewed it, it didn't work. And in that state, it took me only a few hours to work out the beginnings of a new understanding of the Enneagram that now has become so helpful to me. And over time, other extraordinary ideas and visions came to me which showed new aspects. It showed how the triangle worked, in a way that nobody had ever explained before.

I got a flash of something. I saw something like how the cosmoses or the universes move. I realized that this was being *shown* to me, that the active forces were not part of the Enneagram, that they were acting *on* it. They came from above. I can't explain it better than that. Sometimes I would get these flashes and my mind would then take a period of time to work them out, but the flashes came in that state.

There's this idea that there's something so subtle that we don't see it. There's a story where Mullah Nasr Eddin comes upon a group of men standing by a riverbank. They are moaning and crying and bewailing the fact that one of their group was missing and must have drowned. The mullah asked what happened, and they replied, "We don't know what happened. We were ten when we crossed, now we're only nine." And one of them counted, pointing to his peers one by one, "1, 2, 3, 4, 5, 6, 7, 8, 9."

And another agreed with the first, "That's our problem," and he also counted his peers, "1, 2, 3, 4, 5, 6, 7, 8, 9."

The mullah said, "Well, I can return your lost fellow."

They said, "What do you mean? How could you do that?"

He said, "I have certain powers. I can return him."

They said, "You do that, and we'll be in your debt."

The mullah said, "Okay, stand over there," and he counts them, "1, 2, 3, 4, 5, 6, 7, 8, 9, 10."

And they kissed his feet and they thanked him; he had returned their lost friend.

There are always stories about something that's so obvious it's invisible.

There's also a very old story about an Eastern businessman who conducted a business deal in India and was setting out on foot to the next village. A thief saw him do the deal, and that he tucked this big roll of money away. So the thief pretended he was also a merchant, and he said to the businessman, "Let's travel together. It's very dangerous, there are many thieves on the journey."

So they travelled together and came to the inn where they would stay the night. The thief said, "Look, instead of getting separate rooms, why don't we save money and share a room?" So they did. Meanwhile, the thief watched very carefully. And the next morning when the merchant went out to pay, the thief saw that he was only wearing a robe. He certainly didn't have the money on him, so the thief searched everything, all his bags, under his pillow, under the mattress, but he couldn't find the money. He said, "Well, I'll get it. Maybe he's hidden it somewhere on himself."

The next day they travelled again, and again they came to an inn, and in the morning the merchant got up and said, "I'm going down for breakfast. Do you want to join me?" And the thief said, "No, no, no, I have things to do," but gave him a hug, feeling him all over, and thought, "He certainly doesn't have the money on him." So, again, the thief looked through the merchant's clothing, under the mattress, under the pillow, all over the place. He couldn't find the money.

They finally arrived at their destination and the merchant said goodbye, but the thief said, "Wait a second, I have to confess, I'm not a merchant, I'm a thief." He said, "I saw you make a deal. I saw you put the money away. I've been trying to steal your money. I looked under the bed, I looked through all your clothes, I looked under the mattress, under the pillow, I looked through your bags – I couldn't find it. It's driving me crazy! Where could you possibly have hidden it?" He said, "If you tell me where you hid it, I swear I'll go straight, I'll never steal again."

The merchant said, "That's simple. I hid it under *your* pillow."

There's story after story like that and I believe they're talking about the energy of H24. It's there, but nobody sees it. Maybe it is that personality cannot see it because, as I said, personality is not triadically related to H24.

I believe this *has* been referred to in esoteric language. Nobody's ever explained the Holy Ghost. According to my Enneagram, H24 is not self-remembering; *it's what brings you to self-remembering.* There is this preparatory energy that isn't self-remembering itself, but perhaps without it you can't remember yourself, or can't remember yourself intentionally, often enough. And our question is not how to create it but how to relate to it. When Mme. de Salzmann brought centering, people like Mrs. Sutta, at that time, didn't accept it as a Work of Gurdjieff's; she thought it was Mme. de Salzmann's own version. A few *did* accept it. Bill Segal did, I know, and other people. First, in the sittings themselves; these were forty-five-minute guided sittings. She would bring us to this place, this void, that didn't have any personality content, didn't exist with a materiality available to our senses. We would be trying from our mind, our feelings, our body, and I don't believe that any of those centers can go there. We would have that centeredness for a moment. She was trying to get us to open up to that more and more; that was the struggle. We'd begin with the mind, but eventually there has to be a shift. It comes, and then you start to understand how to separate the two, the mental or the emotional, and how to move into this new place.

Mme. de Salzmann gave us all kinds of work and ways to try to help us with this work on centering. I remember once having something I couldn't get past in my emotions, and I remember telling her, "I find a barrier in my emotions." And she said, very simply, "Sense your feet and come to the center from below." And, you know, it worked for a period of time. Mme. sometimes said, "Come from the top," or "Be there quicker than the mind." I asked, "What do you mean, be there quicker?" She said, *"Beat it,* be there before the mind." She brought that for a period of time, and it also worked. Using various techniques, openings appeared and also the features in us. All features are barriers to centering, including chief feature. This was during the sittings. Through struggle these features slowly eroded and started to weaken or fall away for a period of time.

She started to have us bring centering into life. I feel this is where the work of participation was introduced. Once, we were asking questions about being centered, and she gave us a very graphic example. She said, "You're walking down the street, and you pass an ice cream shop. You love strawberry ice cream, and faced with strawberry ice cream, you know you have to have it. You don't deny yourself. You don't say, "No, I'll go against it." You go and buy that ice cream, and when you eat that ice cream, you really eat it with relish, you taste it, but the whole time you're centered, always with attention."

It wasn't just ice cream; you're not going to eat ice cream all the time. I passed a beggar asking for money, so I reached in my pocket and I took out a quarter, dropped the quarter in his cup, and turned away. I was centered, and I started to see an onslaught of "Did people notice me? I gave a guy a quarter! You know, I'm a good guy after all. Who saw me?" All these things started to fill me, and I participated with them; I wasn't taken. Normally I would *be* those thoughts, but I was smiling, laughing, "What a joke! Here I am, trying to have a moment of pure giving. I couldn't even have a minute of pure giving without all of this inner considering suddenly taking over and corrupting it." That's one way we were trying.

During this time, Mrs. Sutta had retired and Christopher Fremantle was taking the group. We kept complaining to him about the fact that we really couldn't bring centering into life. It was hard enough to do it in sittings. One day, he invited six or seven of us to be in a special weekly meeting. He said, "Mme. de Salzmann asked me to bring you this work that she'll bring later in the year to everybody." He told us not to speak about it because at that time we would be the only ones doing it. And the work was to try to be centered; you struggle, and then, at a certain moment when you feel prepared, you begin to risk speaking about it, not from your mind, not from a second before, not from a second after, only *in the moment*. You can describe what's happening, but as you speak, your attention will jump; it will shift; it will move. Don't try to change it. Keep struggling to be centered. Describe exactly what's taking place. So we would try that with Christopher, and the moment we spoke about even a second before he would stop us: "No, that's the past." The moment we'd talk about the future, he'd say, "No, that's the future. *Now!*" This became what we now call Work in the moment. I felt it was a great help in bringing the Work into life because it was teaching me how to follow being centered, watching how my attention was taken and speaking about it, sensing my voice, and speaking about what's taking place only in the moment. This produces a very strong energy even if you're not centered, the demand to be in the moment that way. We were even warned, "Don't do it for that result. You'll get energy from this but don't use it for your 'Work fix.'" Work in the moment is to be used to further bringing centering into life. I believe it is the equivalent of bringing hydrogen 24 into life. It's not enough to just touch it. One must learn how to maintain efforts of work and centering, as well as hydrogen 24, in life. Life will always step on your pet corns, which will always provoke personality into acting, because you have this other energy and personality tries to hide from it. This is part of the *science* of the Work; it's intentional!

A lot of the work in groups is in maintaining an effort, participating, rather than just making an effort to interfere. At the beginning we speak of poking a stick into the spokes of spinning wheels just for a second. That's enough to get a glimpse. But as we get older in the Work, it's not enough. We have to *maintain* struggle; you must be able to maintain it long enough so that struggle in life can do its work.

So that's the history of some kinds of work, like work in the moment, which—tragically, I believe—is now dominating the New York work and being spread around Israel (and certainly other places) like a virus or a plague, because more and more groups and places are working *only* that way due to the influence of some people who don't see any other way of working. It's very easy to be a group leader and say "Work in the moment." And in most of the groups I've visited, people wouldn't even be speaking from the moment. There wasn't a Fremantle saying, "Wait, you're in the past," or "You're in the future." Some groups are more disciplined, but even then, many don't know anything about centering, much less about hydrogen 24. So at best, it turns into, "I feel the air on my skin, it's nice, I feel the sensation, I feel it, and I feel the energy in the room" and if you're honest and you're really connected with watching in that way, there's a demand to be present that does bring in energy. But as I said, from what I understood, "It's not about the energy; it's about the maintenance of effort."

Centering in the life of the body is the beginning of separation from my personality. From this place I can see my slavery more objectively; a new, more objective center can appear. Centering can weaken and demagnetize my personality from the centers. Mme. de Salzmann said that this work on centering was brought by Gurdjieff "only at the stage when one could have a certain kind of 'inner traveling' that's not of the centers, where the centers can't go." Free attention has a different sense of I; it allows me to touch the void.

I remember reading from ninth-century Chinese Buddhist Master Huang Po saying: "Mind is like the void in which there is no confusion or evil, as when the sun wheels through its shining upon the four corners of the world. For, when the sun rises and illuminates the whole earth, the void gains not in brilliance; and when the sun sets the void does not darken. The phenomena of light and dark alternate with each other, but the nature of the void remains unchanged."[2]

By starting to separate consciousness from thought, and freeing attention from attraction and the path of least resistance, it's possible to practice a work that allows me to find a new place in myself that is different than any place I've ever known. The mind can know about it, the emotions can feel for it, the body yearns for it, but one can't get there without free attention; it's only when I've disentangled from the magnetism of the contents of my centers that I can have this free attention. I say all this with a warning: You don't want the mind to take this work. It can never enter this place, and you don't want to give the search to the mind. Even though I'm speaking about this, it can be dangerous. We don't usually speak about it until

---

[2] *The Zen Teaching of Huang Po: On the Transmission of Mind*, translated by John Blofeld, New York: Grove Weidenfeld, 1958.

you're ready for it. It's not going to come accidentally. Many exercises can help lead you there.

The work on centering is a long practice. It takes a long time to even know it exists, even though you keep trying. The materiality of the new center of gravity is so fine that I can't perceive it as I am. The finer the vibration, the less perceptible it is, especially with my other centers manifesting individually, un-unified. Let's say the first note of its octave is silence, void, emptiness. Now, I'm empty, so how can I be there, right? This is where the center of gravity of my attention needs to settle and come to rest. This space is what needs to be occupied. You need a place from which to participate in your search.

I need to be willing to die to the formations of my habitual structures, feelings, and postures in order to shift my attention to this nothingness, or void. This struggle deposits a finer demagnetized energy of the centers, which can flow through the whole body. In the Enneagram it would be the energy of hydrogen 24. In the first triad, it is succeeding higher H24. H24 is invisible to personality because it's not triadically related to H192. But if you struggle in the right way, drop by drop, you start to accumulate these finer vibrations, this finer materiality, and at a certain point there is a shift and this new center of gravity can exist. There's no doubt this place exists, but nobody can say when the shift will occur. It's the center, the hub of this new circulation, bringing unity and a new kind of observation that can see what interferes with unity. It's through this struggle that you start to see deeper features that stop you from being unified. Chief feature is the chief obstacle to moving into this new place because chief feature is the center of gravity of personality. It will always interfere with centering. Think of it from the point of view of the law of Triamazikamno: You need three forces. Where's your holy affirming, holy denying, and holy reconciling? Even after the centers unify they're not the active force; they're not the higher. The higher exists in this new center of gravity which could be receptive to the higher intellectual and the higher emotional centers. The new unity of the lower centers needs to blend with this new center of gravity so that together they reconcile at the higher emotional center. Then, that higher emotional center, which will reconcile at *La* H24, can receive the higher intellectual center which is at H6. That is why consciousness is higher than essence, which is H96.

This work on centering made an extraordinary impression on me! Not right away, but after struggling for a few years, there was a shift. I remember vividly when I had that real shift for the first time. It was the first moment in my life that I was without fear. I saw that my whole life had been based on fear without me knowing it. I'd heard Mme. de Salzmann say "Underneath everything was fear," and I didn't quite believe it until that moment when my attention shifted to a place I never knew before. It was like coming home, so I can't say I never knew it. But it was the first time that I knew I could face anything, even death, from this place without fear! At that moment, I knew this was a very special work. I believe this is the real meaning of the Garden of Eden. As I struggled, slowly tensions started to leave, sometimes violently. As the tensions holding the breath let go, I was actually frightened. My chest and stomach were bouncing in and out involuntarily, a very scary experience. I thought I would have to go to a hospital. Then I realized these were tensions letting go, tensions I may have had for my whole life. As I was opening up to this new passageway I came to this place where my pelvic muscles would relax and just walking became extraordinary. It allowed, not only observations, but I also started to see the obstacles to getting there. It may be that the soul is born in this place. The location of this place of rest or this new center of gravity is different for different people. For some, this place was above the navel and for others it was lower. It was easier in Mme. de Salzmann's presence because of the special energy available when you were with her.

"When a monkey throws a coconut
at a wise man,
instead of throwing it back,
he drinks the milk, eats the meat,
and even makes a bowl out of the shell."

12

Autobiographical material

JERRY'S WORK EXPERIENCES

12.01 Q: Please explain how you understand the ways that the teachings should be exposed to people outside the Work.

JB: I feel that too many people think of bringing the Work the way it was brought at the time of Gurdjieff. Since then the world has changed from the point of view of esoteric knowledge, or spirituality, especially in the West. It seems the materiality of the world is moving east, and the spirituality of the East has moved to the West; but as with many things, as it spreads, it becomes trivialized and weakens.

When I came into the Work in 1953, these ideas were shocking and innovative. When I read the idea of many I's, I was shocked. The ideas fit my experiences, but it had never been formulated in a way that was so clear. And in reading Gurdjieff's ideas, I knew this is what I'd been searching for my whole life, and I was very fortunate to find it.

The Work originally was brought by first studying the ideas. With the study of the ideas we were given tasks to turn the ideas from theories into real experiences. It's one thing to know you're asleep, and it's another thing to experience your sleep. It's one thing to know about many I's; it's another thing to experience many I's. It's the same with considering, buffers, impressions, self-remembering, etc.

I saw that the role of the group leader—and came to understand this later, when I became a group leader—was to take each person's experience and connect it with the proper ideas. Gurdjieff is quoted in *In Search of the Miraculous* as saying, "Unless you connect your experience with the exact right ideas, it invariably will be lost." It's very important to file these experiences in the right place, because it's not just one experience. They need to accumulate like a jigsaw puzzle: piece after piece comes together until they form a picture. The emphasis, instead of being on the ideas, needs to be on having experiences. When I struggle with the task of being present at 10:00, 12:00, and 2:00, I start to see immediately that not only am I asleep but when I wake up at 6:00 that night and realize that I didn't exist all day, it's shocking. So I start to understand that Gurdjieff was very kind when he used the word "sleep" when I realize I've been in a virtual coma, all the time pouring out energy through postures, tensions, and worries. When I actually see it, when I actually experience it, these tensions let go. When people work for a long time and have experiences, they start to understand that the inner world and the outer world are very different than they imagined them. Through this kind of effort, people start to realize that they don't really know or understand the ideas, and as a result, become more interested in them. And we've got to begin to understand these laws because we live under them.

I think a real esoteric school at certain times needs an inflow of new people and it's important. I had an experience a number of years ago when I became involved in starting a new group in Connecticut. It was a great effort for me and several of my older students. I was asked by the Foundation council, "Jerry, why are you doing this? What do we need new people for?" I was shocked! This is a work of transformation, and you can't know how far somebody will go. Some of them will leave, others will move further up the ladder of awareness and maybe take responsible roles. And maybe one of them will be the next patriarch or matriarch of the Work, or will change the Work in a way that makes it actualize its aims. Our role has to be to serve that and not be satisfied with what has become comfortable.

I've given a number of lectures and talks on the Work to people in life and had people come up to me afterwards and said, "I've been doing yoga," or "I've been meditating," or "Oh, what you're talking about is so wonderful. I read about it on the Internet." I realized they're hearing these ideas in the context of what they already know, and they're not hearing the extraordinary miraculousness of Gurdjieff's ideas, which are really very different. Gurdjieff brought a new impulse to the world, maybe for the first time in thousands of years, in the line of Pythagoras, Socrates, maybe even Moses and Christ. Instead it's being heard in the way of New Age ideas and ideas of self-improvement, etc. Now it's even more difficult to shock people. Trungpa Rinpoche called America "the supermarket of spiritual ways." With the ideas being everywhere in a trivialized form, the shock is lost. The Work faces this question of how to deal with renewing the ideas for people of today's world. How do we bring these ideas and methods to people in a way that would be shocking again? I think there has to be a new approach.

I think that there has to be a movement of spirituality towards science, and science towards spirituality. What is spirituality? What is a higher nature? What does it mean to be more conscious? One big question facing the Work: What is necessary to get people to be open to a new way of thinking about these ideas? There has to be a new formulation. I believe the Enneagram that I've evolved is the Enneagram Gurdjieff never completely explained which brings everything in the whole Work together. Will this help bring the Work to a wider world, including the world of science?

I experiment again and again to try to bring the Work out in new and different ways, and giving talks is part of it. The difficulty we see is that no matter what takes place in the world, only a certain number of people come to the Work. When the movie *Meetings with Remarkable Men* was released, Mme. de Hartmann and I were talking about what some people in the Work worried about, that the Work would be overwhelmed by people coming in. Mme. de Hartmann said, "Jerry, don't worry about it. There are the same amounts of people no matter what." And it's true. There are a certain number of people with a magnetic center, and our question is: How do we reach *these people*? There are more than enough; more than that are not needed. We don't need to take people without a magnetic center or to try and develop a magnetic center in people. That might destroy the Work; their values may be of too low a vibration. The current approach isn't attracting enough of the *right* people.

12.02 Q: We'd like to talk about your history in the Work. How did you find the Work? And Mme. de Hartmann wasn't a group leader, so how did you manage to work so closely with her?

JB: I look back on that as almost a miracle because of where I was, where I lived, what I was doing. This was before the Work had the Foundation in New York, and groups met in different people's apartments.

I was a jazz musician in those days, or trying to be. I was relatively young and lived for what was then called bebop, or modern jazz, which was very unpopular at that time. Later, it became *the* jazz. All my friends were musicians and involved with this kind of music. We'd find each other and play together because we loved it. I had been living in the West Bronx, where I was born, but the music scene was in the East Bronx, more of a ghetto-type area, and one had to be pretty streetwise to get around and survive there. I was living for music, but it got a little too hectic. It was at the time that heavy drugs like heroin came onto the scene, and my closest friend at the time died from a poisoned shot of it. I took one look at that and decided this is not for me. I left that scene and went back to the West Bronx, moved back home, and began to hang out at a coffee shop right next to a school with a bunch of fellows and girls that I knew. Many times they would be talking, and I would walk over, and they would suddenly stop talking. I'd overhear little things like "many I's," "negative emotions," things like that, and I started to get very curious. I tried to stimulate them to tell me about it, but they refused. They said "No, you wouldn't be interested." But I kept insisting, and one fellow there with whom I was very close finally told me that two of the boys were actually involved in a thing called the Gurdjieff School, and that they were studying with a woman who had worked with Gurdjieff and Ouspensky. I said, "I would really like to be involved in

166

it," and they said, "Well, it's not so easy to get into. Why don't you read this book *In Search of the Miraculous*?" At that time there was only one bookstore in New York that was selling it. I went and got a copy, and after I got about two-thirds through it, I said, "Look, this is really getting interesting." I'd already told them these ideas were fascinating to me, even before I started the book. One of my friends said, "Well, write the publisher. You have to find your way to it yourself."

So I wrote the publisher and told my friend. He said, "Okay, if you wrote the publisher I'll get you an appointment with Mrs. Evelyn Sutta." At my first meeting with Mrs. Sutta, she had me sit there and wait a while, listening to Gurdjieff's music on this old 33 1/3 LP. They had private copies of it, I think. After we talked, she said, "I'll tell you what. Come to the group. Don't say anything for the first few weeks and we'll see. Talk to me after the first meeting."

I still remember my first meeting. I was very tense. I couldn't stop crossing my legs. I felt the tension in my body, and at the end of the meeting, I walked over and she said, "What did you think of it?" I said, "It was very interesting. I'd like to participate." She gave me a task to try. And with the task, she said, "Just try to remember yourself, see what self-remembering is; you've read about it, see if you could get specific, just see what it is." I remember going back home on the subway, standing, holding a strap, trying to work, and I was thinking, "Self-remembering, self-remembering, self-remembering." And suddenly it was as if I woke up, a vivid impression of myself there holding that strap, which I still remember today. I started to go to the group regularly. We were given tasks every week. Mrs. Sutta was an interesting woman. She gave wonderful, remarkable answers. An energy was there that I started to feel, that I needed, because I saw that I couldn't work unless I went to the group meeting. She had been a yoga teacher and had worked first with Ouspensky, and when he died she went to Europe to meet Gurdjieff and worked with him for a period of time. She was a very serious, wonderful woman.

In 1954 the Foundation purchased the building on 63rd Street. I remember being taken there by Mr. Nyland, before any work was done. It was a garage and coach house, and in terrible shape.

167

Foundation members did a lot of work, and it's now a special building. Movements were available to me right from the beginning. My two friends were then going to Mendham, New Jersey, Ouspensky's farm, where there were work days and weekends. Mme. Ouspensky was still alive and I wanted to go there too, but I was told, "No, you're too young in the Work yet. Wait six months or so."

Six months later I first went to Mendham. It was in the middle of the winter and very cold. I was given a job to work with Lord Pentland and Bill Segal, two of the heavyweights in the Work. Our job was to move a very large pile of manure that was frozen stiff. As I said, I was a musician and I hadn't lifted anything any heavier than my saxophone my whole life. I put the pitchfork into the manure but I couldn't get it out. I was looking over at Pentland and Segal, working so fast and moving huge amounts, while I was still on my first pitchfork. And finally, a half-hour or an hour later, with my hands totally bloodied, I realized that the only thing that was stopping me from running down the road at full speed, probably faster than any car could go, was the fact that I would never come back here again as long as I lived! That thought is what held me through the day, the fact that I repeated to myself like a mantra: "I will never come back here as long as I live," got me through the day. Next we had lunch, then questions and answers, and at the end of the day, we finished with a reading. There was a blackboard near the dining area, and if you were coming back the following week, you wrote your name on the board so they could plan for who was coming, and I saw my body get up, walk over to the board, and write my name in while an inner dialogue went on saying, "Are you out of your mind? What are you doing?" As I saw myself writing my name down on this board I realized *something* in me had been fed that had been starving; and it had nothing to do with this personality that hated it or the discomfort or the blisters on my hands. In these conditions something else was being fed; and that part was also being fed by the group and by Movements (in which I was struggling also).

It took me six weeks to get off the manure pile. They really tested me. People would say to each other when they met at lunch or coffee, "What did you do today?" For the next six weeks nobody had to ask *me* that question. I started to go every week. I remember once I worked as a musician until 4:00 in the morning on a Saturday night. I met some girls and partied the rest of the night; finally, I fell asleep. I woke up automatically, something like 7:00 in the morning and started to get dressed, and one of my roommates said, "Where are you going? You just fell asleep an hour ago." "Oh," I said, "I have to go to this farm to work." They thought I was totally out of my mind. Somehow, I got there. I felt that I had to do it. I went to Mendham for seven years, most Sundays, and often for weekends because on Saturday night they would read passages from *Meetings with Remarkable Men* which hadn't yet been published. To hear a reading from *Meetings with Remarkable Men* was an extraordinary event. I'd be exhausted after working hard all day, going into a hot, stuffy room, especially after lunch, and I'd press my fingernails into the palms of my hands to stay awake to hear the reading. And I wasn't alone. People would fall asleep sitting up, and heads would hit the table sometimes. You struggled with it.

After I was in the Work about a year, something took place that had an enormous action on me. In a way it was the worst thing that could ever happen to me, and at the same time it was the best thing that could have happened to me. I had been smoking pot, marijuana, long before I came to the Work. I was brought up in that culture, so to me there was nothing wrong with it. Some people drank. I smoked pot. I'd never smoke before Movements, but occasionally, if I did a little bit earlier, I could see the effect it had on my attention. I never used any heavier drugs, but it was a time when a number of people in the Work were using pot. After a year I went to Mrs. Sutta and said, "Look, very truthfully, I smoke pot, and I just want you to know it. Now, if it's bad for the Work, I'll stop." She said, "Well, I don't know, personally. Let me check and find out." Well, it turned out there were a number of other people who were caught smoking pot, or they told on each other. I got a call to see Lord Pentland, president of the Gurdjieff Foundation, and he said that they'd decided to put me out of the Work for up to seven years, and after, if my life was solid, I could possibly come back. I remember the room actually spinning, and I left. I didn't know what to do. A couple of days later I got a call from Mrs. Sutta. She said, "Mme. de Hartmann would like to see you." And so I went to see her, and she asked me what had happened. I told her, and she said, "Isn't it strange? You're the only one that admitted to it, and you're the one that's getting all the blame. The other offenders haven't been asked to leave the Work. But this is the way it is." She said, "I'll tell you what I'll do; if you follow a number of suggestions that I give you, I will see you on a weekly basis." I said, "What are the suggestions?" She said, "You have to give up cigarettes, and in addition you have to give up all your friends who are not in the Work." At the time I was hanging out with a number of musicians whom I loved and had close emotional ties with. I said, "Well, I'll say goodbye to them." She said, "No, not even goodbye. Also, you have to move from where you are so they can't find you and you have to get a job and give up music." Again the room spun when I heard "give up music." All I could say was, "I'll do whatever you wish." I walked out, took the pack of cigarettes which I'd never been able to stop for more than two hours and threw it away. I was living in an apartment with my friend Alan, who had brought me into the Work, my closest friend until he died, and I told him everything. Mr. Sutta had a building nearby where there was a vacant apartment, so we moved into this other apartment. I sold my horn, my saxophone, didn't say goodbye to my closest friends, disappeared. I did it. Later, somebody once said, "You know, it's like you were asked to die to your life." I didn't think of it that way then. I had no alternative. Whatever was asked of me, I said yes.

Mme. de Hartmann was an extraordinary being, maybe not appreciated in general by people around her in the Foundation. To the group leaders, she was more often an annoyance factor because she brought them to task; she kept them in line, in a sense. It was amazing how sophisticated she really was, considering she was 72 when I first met her. She looked like a movie star. She had been an opera singer and sang beautifully. Sometimes she sang, and it was wonderful. Her husband, Thomas de Hartmann, the famous Russian pianist and composer, was still alive. I remember once getting piano lessons from him because I started to write music and showed him a song I wrote, which was very naïve, but he said, "I'm not supposed to

170

be doing this, but I'll show you a few things." He was also a very interesting man, but Mme. de Hartmann was the one who actually met with me weekly. I met with her every week, and she gave me tasks. I kept a notebook, and I would go home after each meeting and write down everything that I could remember. I told her everything and asked her advice about everything.

Once, during the following winter, my weekly time to see her came. When she opened the door she was in an evening gown. Inside were people in tuxedos, evening gowns, and I think I saw Leopold Stokowski there. And she said, "What are you doing here?" And I said, "Well, this is my time for the meeting." She said, "Oh, that's right." I said, "I'll come back." She said, "No, no, you're right, this *is* the time for your meeting." I said, "Look, I'll come back any time you want." She said, "No, no, it's the time for your meeting. You wait here." She shut the door, and a few minutes later came out in a fur coat, and we went around the corner to a Jewish delicatessen, and for one hour she spoke to me about my work. How extraordinary is that? She left that party that she and her husband were hosting because that was the time for *my* work. I would have come back anytime, but this was how seriously she took these things. She gave of herself. There were many, many instances like this.

At the end of a year, she said, "It's time." She went to the Foundation, what they called Group One, and said, "It's time Jerry came back." I guess it's my karma that the only rule I established was that if you were put out of the Work, it was for a year. I went back to my group, but I was still meeting regularly with Mme. de Hartmann; and I must have started to act arrogant because Mrs. Sutta said to me, "Look, something is wrong. It's not right that you meet with Mme. de Hartmann *and* the group," she said. "You choose. Either you stick with Mme. de Hartmann and no group, or you stay in the group and no Mme. de Hartmann." Again, a tremendous blow because I'd come not only to value what Mme. de Hartmann was giving me, what an example of goodness, but I came to really love her. So I went to Mme. de Hartmann and said, "I've got a big problem. I can't leave the group and I can't leave you." And she said, "Let me talk to Mrs. Sutta and we'll see." Two days later I saw Mme. de Hartmann and she said,

"We've worked it out." She said, "What I told Mrs. Sutta is, I won't speak to you about the Work, but I need help; I'm an elderly woman. We could see each other under those conditions." I started to see Mme. de Hartmann four or five times a week at her apartment. I was serving people that came to visit. I was like a fly on the wall all the time. I would go into this little kitchen with wooden louvered doors, and I could hear everything in the other room. When people visited I'd be washing dishes behind the doors. I'd wait on a stool until the conversation was over before I came out. It could last up to an hour or two, but I could hear everything that was said. Even when Mme. de Salzmann was there, sometimes she'd let me stay. We became very close. I felt I was her spiritual son. She hurt her back once, and she had to lie down for a couple of months and couldn't get out of bed. The novel *Doctor Zhivago* had just come out. I bought it and I read her the entire book over the period of time that she was ill. For me, it was wonderful just to be with her.

If someone in the Work developed a problem with the Work, if she felt they loved the Work, she would then see them for a period of time. An inner circle of people developed, maybe six or eight, and we would have a special Friday night. She would have a dinner and talk, and we'd ask her all kinds of questions. There was no limit to what the conversations would be about.

Around this time I arranged for Mme. de Hartmann to come and visit Mrs. Sutta's group. Everybody, especially all the young people, actually worshipped Mme. de Hartmann. She had been with Gurdjieff since St. Petersburg, but it wasn't just that; she had this special vibration, something extraordinary. At one time I was very interested in ego. I couldn't see my ego. I would ask her questions and she would give me certain tasks, but I couldn't see it. And I would drive her places. I was developing an attitude, an arrogance: I'd be thinking, "I know Mme. de Hartmann. *I* brought Mme. de Hartmann to the meeting!" Once, after bringing her to my group meeting, somebody said: "It's so good that you're here, Madame." And she said, "Well, I'm here, but not for Brewster. For someone like him, I'd never come, but for you and the others, maybe there's some sincerity. I come for that." And after that, every single question was answered with, "But Brewster could never understand this. He's worthless, you know." Every single thing. I was sitting there with the blood pounding in my ears. My face must have been as red as a beet. I was emotionally very upset. And suddenly I thought, "Everything I'm feeling now is ego. She's not trying to insult me. She's showing me my ego." And I started to take in impressions of myself, saw the look on my face, saw the way I was holding myself: all ego! I realized I *had* been arrogant in my group, very arrogant, because I knew Mme. de Hartmann—right after I had come back to the groups, over the next year. She kept going on the entire evening like this. Later, I had to drive her back home, and there was silence in the car for a while. And then she said, "Do you know what I tried to do?" And I said, "I just want you to know, Madame, that not only do I not hold it against you, I thank you very much." And we both laughed, and she saw I could take it. I'm sure she was interested to see if I could take that kind of thing.

Being around Mme. de Hartmann was no picnic because the moment you fell asleep, you paid the price. I remember she had this enormous room and every surface had all kinds of things on it. There wasn't a surface that didn't have many things everywhere; even the wall was filled. One day she said, "Oh, Jerry, get my glasses." I looked around at this huge room thinking, "Where are her glasses?" I looked here, there, everywhere. She said, "You idiot, where are my glasses? Why can't you find such a simple thing?" And on and on, just screaming at me. As time went on I got to a state where she'd say, "Where are my glasses?" I didn't even have to think, or look, I just reached out and my hand knew where they were. I developed the ability to take a photographic impression of everything in the room the minute I walked in! And then she would smile. If you could find them, she'd give me a big, loving smile and warmth. The minute she saw you understood something, she gave you that look. Later, at one point I said to her, "Madame, why is it that you took a guy like me—I was a jazz musician, I wasn't functioning in life—and you gave me so much? You gave me so much time. Why?" She said, "Well, it's very simple, Jerry: it's because you loved the Work." And I realized that was the truth. If you loved the Work, she gave you everything. Mme.

de Salzmann was like that; Christopher Fremantle was that way, Andre Tracol, these giants. I'm sure Gurdjieff was that way. They gave everything if you loved the Work; if you didn't, you didn't get very much.

12.03 Q: How did tasks and the principles of the Work come into play with your relationship with Mme. de Hartmann?

JB: I'll give you another Mme. de Hartmann story about how sometimes miracles take place if you have the right vibration. She wanted to go to India and she had very little money. She had just enough money to support herself. I knew that one of the women who was fabulously wealthy wanted to give her this huge house in Woodstock, but she refused to take it. One day she said, "You know, I need money. People offer me money, certainly, but I don't wish to take it. I want to *make* money. I said, "Okay. What can we do?" She said, "Well, I can do a couple of things. One thing is I sing, and I write musical notation very well. I wrote all of Thomas de Hartmann's scores out by hand. I copy music very well. So get me a job."

At the time I was working a day job I hated. I had given up music. I was lonely too; I had given up my friends, all because of her requirements. But I couldn't stay away from music. I wasn't *playing* but I was writing music, writing songs. I got very interested in musical theater and became good friends with a man who was the cousin of Jerry Herman, who later became one of the major Broadway composers. He wrote *Hello Dolly, Mame, Milk and Honey*, etc. We all used to hang out at a bar called the Showplace. Dom DeLuise was there and a number of people who later did become famous. So I would work all day, have dinner, and then go to hang out with my friends. At that time, we were all talking musical comedy and musical theater, and I was trying to learn as much as possible. And this friend of mine was a lyricist, so we were writing songs together. I thought, "How in the world am I going to find something for Mme. de Hartmann?"

About the third night after she asked this, I sat down at a table with somebody at the Showplace, and he says, "Oh, I've got this big problem, I'm the choreographer for this off-Broadway show. We think it's going to be a big hit, but the composer only writes in one key, and all the parts have to be written for the band. We need the parts transposed and written." I said, "You what?" He said, "Yeah, we need them written out and transposed from this one key." So I said, "It's funny that you say this, I have a wonderful writing ability." I didn't want to tell anyone about Mme. de Hartmann. I said, "I was a musician you know, I wrote a lot of music. If you want, let me do a test to get this job." He said okay, and the next night he gave me some music. I brought it to Mme. de Hartmann and said, "Something turned up magically, we have the possibility of a job copying and transposing a score for all the instruments." She said, "I don't transpose." I said, "I know, but I do." I remember she took a blank sheet of music paper, and using an old-style pen with a nib and a bottle of ink immediately began copying like crazy with the most beautiful, elegant script you could possibly imagine. Naturally, we got the job, there was no doubt. Every night after work I would go to her apartment and give her the music, and she'd copy it. And this went on for about two months. We made a lot of money.

Once, after we had been working for hours, it was 1:00 in the morning and my head was starting to droop. She said, "Oh, Jerry, you'd better go home. We're through for the night." I said, "No, no, we've still got all this work to do." She said, "No, no, don't worry about it. I'm tired too. I can't go on." I said, "But Madame, you know, I can still work." She says, "No, no, you still have to get up in the morning and go to work. Come back tomorrow night." But when I came back the next day there was a huge stack of music paper. She had finished everything, stayed up the night. She had earned the money to go to India.

She guided me in a lot of ways, in the sense of what's important in the Work and what isn't important. It was an example to see the way she worked. I'll give you another story. There was a woman in Lord Pentland's group who appeared somewhat unbalanced and wanted to see Mme. de Hartmann. I was present when Lord Pentland advised her not to see her, saying, "This woman could be dangerous. She's had a nervous breakdown. She could be violent. We don't know." And a few other older group leaders came and said, "You should not see her under any circumstances. We have a little experience with her. She's a very strange woman." And Mme. de Hartmann went against all that advice and agreed to see her. I asked, "Why are you seeing her?" She said, "Look, Jerry, the chances are that I cannot help her, but there is a small chance that I can. And if I can, I must."

I brought the woman to Mme. de Hartmann's apartment, and as I left, I said, "Madame, I'll be back soon." But I wasn't taking any chances. I stayed on her little stoop outside the window. A good thing the window wasn't dark; I would have been peering in to see if there were going to be any problems, and if any cops came by I would have been arrested on the spot! And so an hour went by and finally the woman left. I went back and said, "Well, what do you think?" She said, "There's nothing I can do for her." But what a wonderful example to see the way they gave. They didn't *talk* about giving; they *gave*. We don't realize that Gurdjieff could have withheld a lot of this knowledge and given just a little drop here, a little drop there. But he supported people who loved the Work. This is another kind of mentality and is why it hurts me when I see people who *can't* give like that or *don't* give like that, and yet they gain power. They gain places in the Work and control many things.

One of Mme. de Hartmann's traits was that she didn't trust anyone. She always checked thoroughly on everything. She had learned that people don't do things well and that unless you do it yourself, or watch over it, it usually wasn't done right. *We're not people who are awake trying not to go to sleep; we're people who are asleep, trying to wake up!* One day, Mme. de Hartmann asked someone, "How is this project being done?" They said, "Jerry Brewster's doing it." She said, "Oh, well in that case it's okay." Everybody was stunned because they had never heard her say that about anybody. It would always be, "Check on it," because she knew that that's the way people are; they're asleep. That's when I knew I had *arrived!*

12.04 Q: Would you speak more about your relationship with Mme. de Salzmann and other people who worked with Gurdjieff?

JB: I remember Mme. de Salzmann coming to our groups

from about 1954. She came with Henri Tracol every year and stayed for three or four months. I spent many Thirteenths, Mr. Gurdjieff's Name Day, with her. There would be joy and laughter; there would be conversation, and you could ask questions. My personal relationship with Mme. de Salzmann began during the stage when I started buying art. I was going to Europe at least eight or nine times a year. I established connections, met people, other dealers and the publishers of Chagall and Miro. That's what grew me from a frame shop in the West Village into a Madison Avenue gallery. I bought art in Europe and sold it here. I saw that I had a real *feeling* for it. I had learned from Mme. de Hartmann to take stock of one's life. Maybe every couple of years, I think, "What is my life? What are my aims now?" And I realized at one point that there had to be three aspects to work in life: First, I will earn my living from what I make with my hands; yet there's a limit to what I can make. Then the next stage has to be making my living from buying and selling not only what I make but also what somebody else made by recognizing what's good from what's not good, and then being able to sell it. The third aspect would be that I would make my living off my *conceptions*, the mind, like publishing books of art. I made an international business out of lithograph art suites by different artists, some well known, some not.

The first time I went to Europe I told a few people in the French groups, "I'd like to see Mme. de Salzmann." They told me, "You can't do that, she's much too busy, you can't bother her." I went to Mme. de Hartmann and I said, "You know, I'm going over to Europe." And she said, "Oh, you must see Mme. de Salzmann!" She gave me her telephone number and said, "She would be very interested in how you're working and how the New York groups are." So the next time I went to Europe, I called Mme. de Salzmann. She said, "Ah, yes, Jerry Brewster. Why don't you come over for coffee? It's now Tuesday; come over Thursday at three." She gave me her address and I went over to see her. We had a wonderful conversation. She asked questions about the New York groups, my work, etc., and said, "Please don't hesitate to call me any time you're in Europe." So eight or nine times a year, I would visit with her.

When Mme. de Salzmann visited New York, sometimes she

would just visit separate groups, but other times three or four groups would get together and meet with her. Once, the Young Responsibles, people they thought would become responsible in the Work, of which I was one, were told, "Mme. de Salzmann is forming a special group, and you're to be in the group Friday night at 6:30." At that time, nothing ever took place at the Foundation on Friday night, and when I arrived there were about sixty or seventy people. At the first meeting, Mme. de Salzmann came into the room and sat down. Most of us were all sitting cross-legged on pillows, others on chairs. This was the first *directed* sitting that I know that was given. Maybe there had been some sittings given to Group One or other people, but I think this was the first organized sitting at the New York Foundation. We were sworn to secrecy not to speak about it, even to each other. We felt at the time we were being initiated into something very special. Until then, my morning sittings were ten minutes or fifteen minutes; this was a forty-minute sitting, cross-legged, and I suffered the pain. That was the beginning of twenty years of working on centering with different exercises, finding this place in the abdomen, the void, a place the centers can't go. You had to separate attention or consciousness from the centers to go there. It was very difficult; naturally, we couldn't do it, but we struggled with it.

A year before this, Mme. de Hartmann had given me a task of trying to find a place in the center of my chest, and whenever I worked on myself, that was the place to which I would bring my attention. I had some very interesting experiences with that. I was a little confused, so after the very first sitting I called Mme. de Hartmann and said, "Mme. de Salzmann is asking us to search in a new place, a different place than the one you had been having me work on for the last year." She said, "Well, I couldn't bring you this work before Mme. de Salzmann did, but I wanted to point you in the right direction." Many group leaders didn't feel this was the right direction for the Work. But the group of us that were invited to these Friday night sittings felt differently, so we used to meet privately, not to speak about the exact place in us because we were told not to, but to talk about some of our approaches. This work on centering later turned out to be very important, so we started working on how to bring the centering into life. And later, when I heard that Gurdjieff had told Orage, "The Work is divided into three parts: interference, participation, and experimentation," I realized centering is really a work on participation, *not* the work on interference. That really was important. Later, Mme. de Salzmann changed it to where we started to work on opening to an energy coming from above the head and down the back. Many people came into the sittings only *after* she was talking about the energy coming from above. They missed the earlier work on bringing centering into life.

I remember talking to somebody about tasks and they said, "Oh, Mme. de Salzmann came to our group all the time and she never gave tasks." It's true. When she came to Mrs. Sutta's group she never gave us tasks because she never wanted to interfere with the Work the group leader was bringing, but *in her group she gave tasks*! Actually, very few people know that she had a group. I was part of a team that was doing the history of the Work in America when we interviewed Bill Segal, who was the one who asked her to bring a meditative exercise. Her answer to him was, "I will bring a certain meditation that Gurdjieff *only* did with his oldest people." If you weren't one of Gurdjieff's oldest people, you didn't get this. I also became very friendly with Henri Tracol. He also looked after some of us; he was always wonderful. Later, when we were given our groups, some older group leaders would try to steal them but he was able to stop those "raids."

When Mrs. Sutta became ill, she went to Florida for her health and started groups there. During this time, Mme. de Salzmann sent the Englishman Christopher Fremantle to take over her groups and others in New York. Christopher had worked with Ouspensky in England, later worked with Gurdjieff, and lived in France working with Mme. de Salzmann. Christopher was another one of the people that valued the Work and didn't value position, place, and ego, someone who *served* the Work. A very soft-spoken man, we used to call him a steel hand in a velvet glove. I worked with him, and he convinced me at that time to become a group leader. I started with two elderly ladies and an elderly man, and all the Brewster groups

179

came out of that. Christopher Fremantle came every week to group meetings with me.

Christopher Fremantle and Bill Segal were painters. One day, after Ouspensky had died, they were talking to Mme. de Hartmann, and she said, "You know, you're both artists. Why aren't you painting?" And they mentioned that Ouspensky had asked them to *give up* their art as a task to go against their mechanical nature. She responded, "That's nonsense! Gurdjieff would never ask someone to do that. Temporarily, yes, I could understand giving it up for a certain period of time. But you're artists, so go back to painting. I give you a special task: every Friday morning I want you to leave a painting outside my door." I know this because she asked me to frame the paintings. She had a whole wall of paintings by Fremantle. I don't know what happened with Segal. I never saw his paintings. I don't know if he did the task, but he later went on to become a well-known artist. They were both wonderful artists.

With me, it was a different story. After eight years, one day I was with Mme. de Hartmann, having coffee, helping her some way, and she looked at me with a quizzical look, saying, "Jerry, why aren't you playing music?" I said, "Madame, don't you remember? You asked me to give up music." She said, "That's the past, I wanted to make sure you didn't have a road back to drugs. But it's been eight years. Play!" I went back to music, got back some of my ability, and actually, occasionally, played professionally again for a few years until I felt it was not a right work for me.

Once when I was over for coffee with Mme. de Salzmann in her Paris apartment, she said, "I'd like you to do me a favor." I said, "Anything, Madame, anything you want." She said, "You know, my son Michel doesn't like America, doesn't seem to like Americans. I think that's because he doesn't know enough." She said, "I'd like you to call and meet with Michel when you come next time, tell him about your Work in New York, and about what's taking place in New York, and describe your work, and all of this." Michel was thin and dark haired then; this goes way back. The next time I was in Paris I called Michel, and he said, "Ah, yes, I'm having a special reading at 6:00 in the morning on *Beelzebub*, in French, naturally. Why don't you come to the house and join us?" I remember this clearly; I was so exhausted, I had missed a night's sleep on the plane coming over. I said, "Michel, I don't know if I can come. I'm really in a state of exhaustion, and I've got all kinds of appointments with artists and publishers." He said, "Well, if you can." Naturally, I found myself there at 6:00 in the morning and for an hour listened to *Beelzebub* in French. And then Peter Brook and Michel and I went to a little café nearby. I remember having these wonderful conversations with them. Later, when I went to Michel's place, I told him about my Work and he listened. I didn't know if he was interested at the time. Nobody then had a hint that he would become the Michel that we knew later, another man who gave everything! I believe that my meetings with Michel over the next eight years positively affected his feelings towards America.

The older members of my oldest group and I used to go to Henri Tracol's place at Gordes, which is in the South of France near Avignon. We went there for eleven or twelve years. Later we went to work periods in Chandolin, Switzerland, with Michel de Salzmann. I started to see Michel as an older brother, someone who had something extraordinary and was on his way to becoming a Mme. de Salzmann or even a Gurdjieff. I started to feel that many people in my groups needed this experience, so I once brought twenty-two people. He allowed it; instead of seventy people that time we had ninety or so. I only brought people who were working on themselves and needed the shock of the work period. It was a wonderful period and produced a very fine vibration in all of us. I never tried to hold people back.

The influence of Mme. de Salzmann is so great because she brought lines of Work over long periods of time, and later we realized it all made sense—it's all like a scientific spirituality, a spiritual physics. It was all based on objective science, the laws and the forms which I'm sure she got from Gurdjieff. I'm sure she tried to pass on as purely as possible what she got from Gurdjieff, just as I try to pass on as purely as possible what I got from her.

People who knew Gurdjieff say that you could not even conceive what he was like. But if he was anything like Mme. de

Salzmann, he was quite extraordinary. She was amazing. When you were with her she was never without a certain presence, an inner stability, and a center. You felt that every minute. You never saw her without it, no matter what. You laughed a lot; there was a sense of joy being with her.

12.05 Q: Thanks for sharing those experiences with Mme. de Hartmann and Mme. de Salzmann last week. What other experiences revolved around them?

JB: Mme. de Salzmann had given the Foundation the task of doing the Oriental Street Fair. The whole Foundation was working full time on this. That project has a long history. It was based on a painting by Alexandre de Salzmann. In it he included Gurdjieff, Mme. de Hartmann. Many people in the Work were portrayed. Mme. de Salzmann wanted us to recreate that street scene, and we worked on it for years. Some people were learning Arabic, others studying the costumes. I was in the Middle Eastern band, which was led by a professional Middle Eastern musician. We took this very seriously. We actually sent a man who had perfect pitch and perfect memory of music to Turkey to observe the Mevlevi Dervishes, whose music is very secret. You couldn't bring in the large recorders of the day, and there were no recordings of it. At night he listened to the music while the Dervishes were dancing; then he went back to his hotel room and wrote it all down. We also had him buy certain Turkish instruments. And I ended up with an instrument which is called the *zauna*, which is an impossible instrument for a Westerner to play. But I tried and tried and finally got some ability. We had some long flutes and a number of different instruments. They were all difficult, but the *zauna* especially.

We would meet two or three nights a week in the Movements hall; people would be sewing, and there was a singing group, a dancing group, and our band was practicing these Eastern songs. At one point the band decided to go to Mendham for a week to work out the instruments separately. At that time I developed some kind of infection and the doctor advised me not to go to Mendham, but I said I needed to go, so he gave me a whole bunch of penicillin to take with me. And we did a lot of work and were able to work out a number of songs. I was able to play a number of songs on the *zauna*. It is a very shrieky and powerful instrument. It stood out. It was like a key, the middle element of the sound of the band. We worked and worked, and then gave a concert on the last Sunday. That was the only time I ever heard applause at Mendham. I mean, people sometimes put on shows at special days, but I had never heard applause.

But the whole time my infection was getting worse, and I ended up in the hospital with a fever of 105 degrees, not expected by anyone in the hospital to live through the night! It turned out that the bug I had was impervious to most antibiotics; it was one of the first bugs that came along that was resistant. Fortunately, and the reason I am still here, in the middle of the night the laboratory finally found one antibiotic that worked, and that saved my life. But I was so close to death that I needed a long recuperation period.

Around that time my life changed. Before that I had been playing at a club in the Village once a week. But after getting sick I couldn't play, so at first I'd have replacements come in while I sat around with friends. And once, a very close friend of mine who was a master framer and I had a talk. He was telling me that he found this little basement and he was thinking of opening a shop but didn't have enough money. And I decided that I had had enough of the music world, that playing music was not the work for a real man, too many negative elements. So we decided to become partners. I borrowed some money from family and we opened a basement framing shop in the Village.

We went to the lumberyard to get planks of wood in order to make our own moldings; we'd cut it into strips, and then we'd spend the rest of the night with wood scrapers taking out the burn marks from the saw. For a period of time we were so poor that I had to keep working at music, so I got a job in a club on Bleecker Street, right across from the Village Gate. I played six nights a week so I didn't need to take money from the shop; supporting myself that way allowed us to survive for the first year. At that time I would work downstairs in the basement all day, learning the craft, and then I would go up to Movements or to a meeting; I'd make sure that the Movements and readings were early enough, then take a train down to Bleecker Street, play the first set, at which time I would be starving, and I would then go around the corner to a place called the Hip Bagel, the in spot at that time.

Then the second year we started to make a little money and I was able to leave working at the club, but not the Hip Bagel because I met this waitress who I fell in love with, Joan, a young actress from California, and we got married. However, after three years of marriage even though we loved each other, we decided to break up, as friends, still loving each other.

There's a reason why I am bringing all this background. Joan came into the Work and became very close to Mme. de Hartmann, who saw something very special in her. Joan spoke French fluently, so she used to go to Paris to dub French movies into English, and English movies into French. At the time, Mme. de Hartmann went to live in a suburb of Paris, and Joan moved in with her and helped her. And when I went to Paris, Joan would be my interpreter. It was a very good arrangement.

Mme. de Hartmann was getting old and frail at this time, so when she traveled from Paris, Joan would help her onto the plane in the first row of seats, and I would be there when she arrived in New York to help her from the plane seat right into the wheelchair. (In those days, it was possible to convince the airlines to let you onto the plane.)

During this period I bought out my partner. I found a store for rent only a block away, at street level rather than a basement. And it also was during this period that I saw things about how accumulators worked, and their role relating to the wrong work of centers, and I was able to be free of that and became a craftsman. I felt I could do anything well. Anything I'd touch with my hands became beautiful. So when I opened up the new store I got into buying and selling art.

I was very involved in a big art deal when I got a call from Joan who said, "Jerry, Mme. de Hartmann is coming back to New York next week on the thirty-first and isn't feeling well, and I am a little worried about her. Do you think that you should come to France and take her back?" I said, "It's a very difficult time." She said,

184

"Well, she's not really ill but she's not feeling right." And I said, "Well, ask her about it and we'll see." The next time I talked to Joan she said that Mme. de Hartmann said, "No, you don't need to come," but Joan was still concerned. I started to think about how Mme. de Hartmann had helped me in so many ways. But I also thought, "I'm in the middle of this deal, and besides, we would put her into the first row of seats on the plane, she'd be looked after by the stewardess, and then I would come right into the plane to pick her up. For that six-hour flight there would be nothing I could do that the stewardess couldn't do." I started to ponder, "How could I go over there?" I was torn by yes and no: "Mme. de Hartmann, to whom I owe so much, may need me now," but "even she didn't want me to come over," and "it's only six hours," and "she will be taken care of by the stewardess," and "I'm involved in this deal, and to lose it will be a disaster for me." The impulses on both sides were equal, and for a couple of days I was in torment.

The reason I know the date is that the anniversary of Gurdjieff's death is October 29, and there was always a service performed within a few days at the Russian church on Second Street, between First and Second Avenue. And I went with this question in mind, being torn, sitting there while the service was going on, for about half an hour, every minute thinking, "Gurdjieff, send me a message. I really don't know what to do." All I saw were turning thoughts and agitated emotions. As I walked out of the service I saw Mrs. Howarth, a Movements teacher, who recreated the Movements with Mme. de Salzmann. She was fairly old then, and usually her daughter Dushka or other people would be walking with her, but she was alone and walking towards Third Avenue. And in those days it was a pretty rough area, the upper part of the Bowery, and there were drunks all over the place. I caught up with her and said, "I am going to Third Avenue to get a taxi uptown. Let me walk with you, and we can share a taxi to the Village." At Third Avenue we were waiting to get a cab but there weren't any. Suddenly, a smelly bum came over and in a slurry voice said, "Hey man, give me some money." And I was stunned because when I was playing music, I hung out with this guy; he knew all the places and people in Harlem and we used to go there and play music together. And I looked into his face and said, "George?" We looked at each other, and at that moment, I thought, "This could have been me if I didn't meet the Work." That was the only time I ever saw him. I gave him some money, Mrs. Howarth and I got a cab, and then I suddenly realized, "What could have been a better message than that? There, but for the Work, go I." I realized that I had no choice. I actually did get a message, in a form I could never have anticipated!

So I got on a plane to Paris, and it turned out I had one day there. Going around with Joan, I actually found an incredible business deal with a publisher of a series of Salvador Dali hand-painted etchings, a contact which turned out to be very good for me financially for a long period. And I met Salvador Dali, who gave me a fairly large etching and also did a drawing on which he wrote "Homage to Monsieur Brewster," which I still have. I accompanied Mme. de Hartmann back to New York, and everything went well. But the miracle I've always remembered, how extraordinary a message from Gurdjieff that brought me back to a proper valuation of this woman who saved me in the Work.

There are a couple more stories I could relate that involve Mme. de Salzmann and Trungpa Rinpoche, the Tibetan lama who brought Tibetan Buddhism to America. Trungpa Rinpoche was quite an extraordinary man. Mme. de Hartmann liked him very much, and I used to take her to his talks. A close friend of mine, Michael Cohen, was involved in his teachings and became very close to Trungpa, and was in charge of his work in Europe at one time. Michael was the religion editor for the Encyclopedia Britannica. I think he was the one who originally put Ouspensky's and Gurdjieff's names into the Encyclopedia Britannica.

When Trungpa came to New York, he would stay at a very large apartment around the corner from me. A lot of his disciples would come and there would be parties and talks. Meanwhile, when Michael would visit New York he would stay with me, so I was considered a host, and I was invited to these parties and got to know Trungpa Rinpoche very well. Trungpa had an extraordinary attention, but one of his problems was that he was an alcoholic who

186

drank very heavily, drank himself into oblivion, and he did eventually die from it. I remember once he was to speak at a Unitarian church, and he was already about an hour late; he was so drunk his disciples had to pick him up and walk him to the car. I remember thinking, "How is he going to talk now?" When we arrived he started to walk, staggering a little bit. But as he walked he began to straighten up. Suddenly there was no staggering, and he got up on the podium, and for an hour and a half he spoke so brilliantly, it was unbelievable, generating an energy, speaking about the cutting edge of attention, the sword of attention! Then he walked off, and as he got closer to the car he started to stagger again, and as we got into the car, he was dead drunk. I saw that ability he had for the entering of something into him which was absolutely extraordinary. Back at the apartment, he was out like a light.

There were a number of people among his disciples who had been in the Work. But I realized that everything he knew about Gurdjieff he knew from these people who had left the Gurdjieff Work. I thought, "Somebody has to talk to him who is still in the work, someone who is still positive about Gurdjieff's teachings." So occasionally, when we met I would talk to him about Gurdjieff and the Work. Then, at one point he was going to be on the local PBS TV station for a three-hour symposium with a panel of people high up in the Buddhist movement and Alan Ginsberg as the moderator. I got a call from my friend who said, "Trungpa wants you to be on the panel." I thought, "That's an honor, certainly!" I went into the studio and I was on this panel. Alan Ginsberg asked Trungpa questions first and then it was time for the panel to ask questions, so I asked something about attention. I thought it went very well. Later, we went back, and he drank himself into oblivion again.

The next evening I walked into the Foundation and Lord Pentland was in the foyer waiting for me. His first words for me were, "Brewster, are you a wolf in sheep's clothing or a sheep in wolf's clothing?" I said, "What are you talking about?" He said, "I saw you last night. Don't think you're going to get away with this. I saw you on Channel 13," and he started to berate me! So, we're in this conversation, and he's very aggressive and I'm trying to defend myself, and then the elevator door opened and Mme. de Salzmann comes out, about to leave the building, but she hears our conversation and comes over and asks, "What's going on?" I told her there was a symposium with Trungpa Rinpoche, that I had a friend who was a disciple of his, that I got to know Trungpa very well, and that Trungpa asked me to be on the panel. And Mme. de Salzmann looks at me and says, "How wonderful, you represented the Work last night. I know Mme. de Hartmann likes Trungpa very well. She would have really been proud of you. I feel you really did the Work a service. How wonderful that you could do that." Meanwhile, Lord Pentland was looking on with wide eyes. Mme. de Salzmann smiled and walked out. That ended that. Later, even Lord Pentland got very friendly with Trungpa.

Another story connected with both Mme. de Salzmann and Trungpa makes me feel I influenced him. Trungpa had gotten very popular and written a number of books; he was a superstar on the spiritual scene. When he was in New York he stayed at this apartment, a kind of loft, where they had his groups and was seeing and interviewing people; he had very limited time because there were so many people looking to speak with him. During that time I had been working in Mme. de Salzmann's group on centering. Once, when Trungpa was in New York I went to see him and decided to tell him about my *real* inner work, about exactly what I was doing, centering, how this energy was vibrating in me at that moment. I was looking him in the eye and I could see he was vibrating too, and a tremendous atmosphere sprang up between us, a living vibration. I was in a state of grace, and I explained exactly the work I was doing, exactly the results, how these energies worked in me. And then my time was up and I left.

When I left Trungpa, I was elated. I was in a state of, as I said, grace. And I remember thinking, "God—nothing could top this." That night I had my group meeting with Mme. de Salzmann, and I went into the meeting room and sat down, and after a short while Mme. de Salzmann came in. I was just floating in this energy that remained after my meeting with Trungpa. Then somebody asked a question and Madame started to speak. Within five minutes, the thought in my mind was, "No contest!" Even though she was speaking to everyone, it was it as if she was speaking only to me, to the heart of my work. From what she was bringing at that moment, I started to feel an even higher energy penetrating me. At that moment I became totally convinced about who Mme. de Salzmann was.

There's another offshoot to this with Mme. de Hartmann. Trungpa had set up the Naropa Institute in Boulder, Colorado, and it started to become successful. My friend Mike, who was working there at the time, was getting married there, and he wanted me to be his best man. But there's no best man in the Buddhist ceremony, so I was something like keeper of the seals, and Trungpa actually performed the ceremony. After the ceremony, my wife Sharon and I spent a couple of days in Boulder with Mike and his wife; then they went off to California on their honeymoon and Sharon and I headed to Santa Fe to visit Mme. De Hartmann where she was living at the time .

Mme. de Hartmann had reserved a motel room for us, but when we got there the person at the reception desk said, "I don't see your name here. Are you sure?" I said, "What do you mean?" Mme. de Hartmann told us she was going to arrange the room, and I knew there was no way she was going to screw up! I said, "You've got to look further because I am sure the reservation was made." They said, "We've got a real problem because there's no room." I said, "Well, please look." Finally, it turned out there was a paper with our names written on it that was supposed to have been entered, and somebody missed entering the reservations. So they said, "We'll put you in the bridal suite, and we'll charge you the same price." We said, "Great!" So we found ourselves with a beautiful, huge room with a great view and a sitting room. Then there was a knock on the door, and I said, "Ah, the jig is up. They found another room and they're going to take us out of here." I opened the door, and there was Mike and his wife. They said, "We decided not to go to California but to spend our honeymoon here with you and Mme. de Hartmann." I said, "Well, you know, it's funny, because even though we didn't know that, we have the bridal suite!" So they used one room and we had the other, and we visited Mme. de Hartmann during the day.

As I said, Mme. de Hartmann loved Trungpa. At one point Michael asked Mme. de Hartmann: "We all know the situation with

Trungpa. What do you really think about his drinking and fornicating?" And her answer was, "Look, I couldn't care less about that. He has a right to do what he wants to do. But I do fault him, and the reason I fault him is because of what he does, he will die early. And by dying early, he will not provide you with what you need later, with what you're trying for. He will deprive you of the development, of his presence and his knowledge, that he would keep from you what he could bring you as he got older; for that I fault him." And it's true. Trungpa died early, before he was fifty. When he died, I remembered Mme. de Hartmann's answer, how practical it was.

On another trip to New Mexico, we were out drinking in a Mexican bar, downing tequilas and talking about the Work with Carl Robinson, a doctor into holistic medicine who had been living there. I think his family is in the Work. Then a middle-aged Indian came up to the doorway and said, "Would you mind if I join you?" And I said, "Why do you want to join us?" He said, "I have a farm outside of Santa Fe, and things are bad. I don't have a car now, and a friend of mine is picking me up. He asked me to meet him here, but I see this kind of Mexican bar could be dangerous for me. Indians and Mexicans don't always get along, but I think if I am with you, I am going to be alright." I said, "Certainly, sit down." He joined us and we could see something in him, a simplicity. He said, "I live off my small farm." One of us asked, "How were the crops this year?" He said, "Terrible. We had a big hail storm, and all my crops were wiped out." We looked at him and Sharon said, "You said you lived off your farm. If all your crops were wiped out, how are you going to get by?" He said, "Well, that's what friends are for." Fantastic. Meanwhile, there was such a feeling of peace in him. And then his friend came and he left. This was a true man of essence, and he emanated this vibration that we all felt, a sense of joy, a sense of life.

Being around Mme. de Hartmann, seeing her three or four times a week, sometimes talking with her on the phone every day was a relationship that had a work element but also a life element to it, an interaction. With Mme. de Salzmann it was different. It was purely a work relationship; if you loved the work and you worked on yourself, she was open to you and gave in a way that was really quite extraordinary, a way that you don't find in life. Experiences I had with Mme. de Hartmann are often stories, and with Mme. de Salzmann it's more work experiences, and occasionally very interesting personal experiences. One such story is very close to me. I mentioned that I went over to Paris eight or nine times a year, and each time I would see Mme. de Salzmann. One time there, we were talking, and I started to see something about myself that I had never seen before. Every subject that was brought out, like when she would bring up a subject about art, I would talk about *my* art and what *I* did. Whatever the topic, I would bring it back to *me*; *I* became the center of the subject whenever I spoke. Mme. de Salzmann was seeing me, accepting me, "That's part of Brewster." She wasn't judging; she was like a mirror. I saw that I turned towards *me*; I had to be the center of every subject. I couldn't stop it and it became unbearable after a while. The strange thing is, I saw it and said, "I am not going to do it," and the next thing I knew, I was doing it again. It probably had always been like that.

When I got back to New York, every single time I thought about what I saw, my skin crawled. It wasn't that I *remembered* the situation; I *relived* it. This went on for months. I would see Mme. de Salzmann in my mind's eye and I'd feel myself doing it, then organic shame. But on my next visit with Mme. de Salzmann in Paris it wasn't there anymore. I was actually able to have conversations I didn't have to be the center of. We had a wonderful *conversation*, without it being just about *me*, and the conversations went further with a lot of laughter and joy. What a feature that was, invisible to me my whole life, and even when it became visible, unstoppable for so long. Once I was free of it, it enabled me to relate to her as a human being, to be present in front of her without that filter. My wish for you would be that you too experience this one day yourself.

"The Enneagram I'm bringing has allowed me to relate experiences that I had in my years in the Work. It's not just theoretical. Entering the Enneagram I become aware of myself. Self-observation is the characteristic of that note. In formatory apparatus, I'm not in the Enneagram."

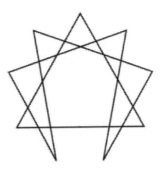

"In order to understand the enneagram it must be thought of as in motion, as moving. A motionless enneagram is a dead symbol; the living symbol is in motion."

13

MY NEW UNDERSTANDING OF THE ENNEAGRAM

JB: For those of us who are in the Work, the purpose of the Enneagram is to show us where we are at all times in our inner search. It's a map. It shows me where I am and where I need to go. The main difficulty is to maintain objectivity about where I really am. The Enneagram can help me with this as I experience and understand the vibrations that pass through me and their relationship to each other. Everything, everywhere, space, "emptiness" is filled with vibrations; we live in a sea of vibrations. What we call empty space in our universe is filled with vibrations from cosmic rays to radio waves to Wi-Fi. If you have the right receiver, you can get South Africa, China, or Norway right now, here. You are not calling the waves: *they are already here*; all we have to do is be receptive to the right frequency. All vibrations are under the law of octaves, and all vibrations react triadically. I believe that each center is part of a large octave and that each center also has inner octaves, like a piano, C to C, *Do* to *Do*. Depending on the scale, all *Dos* have the same characteristics, just like each octave's *Re, Mi, Fa, Sol, La*, and *Si* will have the same characteristics.

The hydrogens in the Enneagram are used simply to show scale. Mr. Gurdjieff used them in the Food Diagram and in the Ray of

Creation. For example, in the Food Diagram he said that H96 represented rarified gases. In the Ray of Creation, H96 represented the number of laws under which one lives according to where they are in the universe.

In my Enneagram of Change of State, H96 represents essence; and in my Enneagram of Level of Being, H96 represents the level of one's being. These hydrogens can represent scale, frequency of a wave, rate of vibration, or level of being, depending on the context. There of course are parallels, but these must be carefully studied and experienced to be understood.

Here's what I mean by that: Let's say the thinking center has the idealized vibration of H48, but the center also has inner octaves of H384 up to H6. H384 would be total fantasy, dreaming, and uncontrolled turning thoughts. One of the general characteristics of H384: *it always gets the opposite of what it wants and expects.* At H192, there are the associations, my education, and my formatory thoughts. At H96 it would be more essential, a quieter mind. It would be coming up with solutions to problems. At H48 it would be what Zen calls "no-mind": I still have associations, but they're quiet. At that level, you might realize that associations are one of the greatest gifts that were given to us because they're quiet, ready, and anything you need comes wrapped up—all the connections known, better than any computer, even things you didn't know you knew. Living without turning associations is difficult at the beginning because our conceptual I is so connected with these associative and formatory thoughts; but when we get past that difficulty we start to love being open, taking in impressions. And then there is the thinking of H24—more conscious, the kind of thoughts an Einstein or Newton might have had. And then there's H12, which could be ideas on the level that Gurdjieff brought. And maybe at H6 you have the mind of Earth; Edgar Cayce reportedly would access a state where he could *see* everything on earth.

It's the same with the physical body. That center, let's say, is idealized H24. What would be the characteristics of the inner octaves of H24? It would start with H768 down to H384; within this range there could be physical damage and people could have had tensions for so long they've developed a hunchback because of their posture. At H192 there would be postures and tensions connected with identification not being connected with gravity; being connected with the identifications associated with these postures take you out of the body and its connection with gravity. At H96, which is more essential, with the sensation of a flow of energy and freedom of movement, you now could be connected with gravity; you sense the alignment of the spine one vertebrae on top of the other. At H48, one's aim is consciousness: one is much more aware; one would have sensation. At H24 you would sense the instinctive center; you would sense vibrations moving through the body, what I call resonance; it may be the source of what is called *chi* energy. In the physical body at H12, it's sexual energy—a very high vibration, higher than the basic fuel of the body. This would now be part of the miraculous; this doesn't occur naturally.

The same process with emotions: they start with H12, but the inner octave has a range starting with H384, and again, each of these has certain specific characteristics. At H384 maybe you're in a rage all the time; at H192, worry, anxiety, stress, and negative imagination. Someone asked Gurdjieff, "How could I love my enemies?" He replied, saying, "That is not your problem. Your problem is you can't love your friends." That's personality. It remembers it once loved, it has a feeling, but it's in memory. At H96 the emotional center would be feeling joy; we could love our friends. For a man of H48, emotions would be the beginning of a love of consciousness, awareness, joy at being in the moment. At H24 there's unity, and maybe real love. There's where you *could* love your enemies. At H12 there would be faith, love, and hope: conscience. And at H6, certainly, you would be Man No.7; it would be the highest that one could achieve.

And there is also the sexual center, which has this same range of hydrogens. One of the characteristics of H384: *it always gets the opposite of what it wants and expects.* H384 could be sadomasochism instead of pleasure; it's fantasy or pain that connects with the sexual energy. At H192, which is "regular" personality, the sexual energy is not vivid, not intense; one is driven by it, certainly, but it's usually not deep or pleasurable, not connected with the whole body. At H96, or essence, it would be more like three-centered sex. We don't realize that a lot of sex is one or two-centered. Then there's H48, the sex of Man No. 4, which is more conscious sex, where the sexual energy becomes something that joins one's presence; one is not asleep while having sex. You receive the impressions of it. At H24 you're free of all the mechanical, accidental education; the energy stimulates the acts rather than the acts stimulating the energy. At H12, it could be conscious sex, in which the higher centers would be involved. And certainly at H6, it's something that I couldn't describe.

What are the laws connected with the Enneagram?

The law of three and the law of seven are the two laws that move the Enneagram towards evolution. I believe that the law of three is the basic law of the universe. Everything in the universe relates triadically to the "motor" that causes movement in the universe. The law of seven describes how it moves. There are two ways that it moves. One is the descending, involutionary movement, which Gurdjieff calls the "Ray of Creation" of the material universe. Everything becomes more and more dense. It is strange that Gurdjieff called it the ray of creation because everything becomes more mechanical and comes under more laws. The ray of creation starts with 1; it meets 6and becomes 3. 3 is the middle. It meets 12 and becomes 6, and then continues its descent. If there is a descent, there must be a return—an ascent. But you go down a steep hill differently than you go up a steep hill.

The other movement is the evolutionary movement. It implements the law of Triamazikamno, the law of three: the higher blends with the lower in order together to actualize the middle, and thus, to become either higher for the preceding lower or lower for the succeeding higher, which I believe is the movement shown by the Enneagram. In *In Search of the Miraculous*, the forces are called active, passive, and reconciling, or neutralizing. In *Beelzebub*, Gurdjieff brings the formula stated above, and in my opinion, that's as important to the spiritual world as $E=mc^2$ is to physics.

I have personally come to believe through what I've discovered that a more precise knowledge of the laws is necessary.

What really needs to take place is to bring the law of three to the law of seven. Not just as a beginning it applies to every movement and every moment. I read in Maurice Nicoll's *Commentaries* that the ascending, or the evolutionary, octave begins with a passive *Do*. The Enneagram is not just a symbol, but in reality it's an instrument, like the microscope, to examine anything you wish to examine based on transformation. Gurdjieff said in relation to this: "All knowledge can be included in the enneagram and with the help of the enneagram it can be interpreted. And in this connection only what a man is able to put into the enneagram does he actually know, that is, understand. What he cannot put into the enneagram he does not understand. For the man who is able to make use of it, the enneagram makes books and libraries entirely unnecessary. Everything can be included and read in the enneagram."[1]

So the struggle they were making to understand was one that Gurdjieff *wished them to try*, rather than to accept these ideas passively. They had to really struggle to understand what were and still are very new ideas. The Enneagram, as brought in *In Search of the Miraculous*, was brought that way and then never really continued. There's also a place in *A Further Record* where Ouspensky gives a talk on the Enneagram in 1938 and said, "I gave more in this group first time that I spoke than we had in Petersburg." Now, many entire books have been written about the Enneagram by both people who have been in the Work and many who never were—all based on the Enneagram in *In Search of the Miraculous* which doesn't quite work! In my opinion, all of this interpretation doesn't make sense, doesn't mean anything, because *Gurdjieff disguised the Enneagram*!

As I was studying the Enneagram, a new movement appeared to me. Later I was explaining it to someone in the Work I'd known for a long time, and he asked me a very good question: "If what you're saying is true, why did Gurdjieff bring it in that way?" I thought, "Good question." I mean, it's true, right? And yet I was so convinced that the one in *In Search of the Miraculous* doesn't work that I would go to bed at night saying, "I really found the real Enneagram. It's hard to believe." And I'd wake up in the morning saying, "Am I out of my[3] mind? I really think I found the real Enneagram? I must be crazy! What a weird dream!" But I would go back to my notes and look and say, "My God!" I would see the movement; I would feel this new dimension again. Every time I would work on it, I would uncover new material. It was like reading a new book. I went back to *In Search of the Miraculous* to reread from where he quoted Ouspensky and asked that question about the Enneagram. And what did I find? I found these phrases: "And if it now is, so to speak, made available to all, it is only in an incomplete and theoretical form of which nobody could make any practical use without instruction from a man who knows." "If you think I'm bringing you the real Enneagram, you're mistaken. This Enneagram is of no value and will bring you nowhere."[1] And when I went back to my friend, he too was quite amazed because he too didn't even remember those phrases. I believe the Enneagram as presented in *In Search of the Miraculous* is incomplete and it actually has a different movement altogether.

In the figures which follow, when H appears before a numeral it refers to the hydrogen at that point.

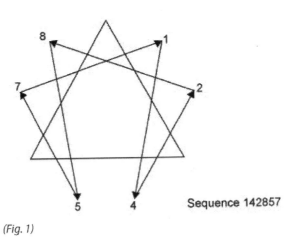

Sequence 142857

(Fig. 1)

What is the real movement in the Enneagram? Gurdjieff brings out the idea that it's based on 1, 4, 2, 8, 5, 7, the sequence of numbers that result from 1 divided by 7. (See fig. 1.) In Movements, many of the[ii] sacred dances, especially the multiplications, are based on this 1, 4, 2, 8, 5, 7 movement.

You have to get into the Enneagram, and you have to get out of the Enneagram. Ordinary man in life is not in the Enneagram; he is under the law of accident and following the path of least resistance. What are the requirements for entrance into the Enneagram? I realized that in the Enneagram, we are dealing with two triads, right and left. There are actually three, but the third triad will not be covered in this introduction. The shocks are located on the triangle and the triangle moves counterclockwise H6, H24, H96. (See fig. 2.)

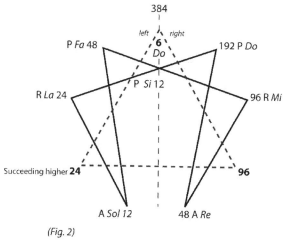

(Fig. 2)

The movement of the first triad requires active *Re* H48 being brought to passive *Do* H192 and reconciling at *Mi* H96. The shock of succeeding higher H24, from the triangle, brought to H96 on the right side of the Enneagram transforms and moves the energy of reconciled *Mi* H96 into a passive *Fa* H48 on the left side.

With the shock, passive *Fa* H48 is produced, which is the movement *towards* the left triad (the evolutionary movement). Passive *Fa* H48 interacts with active *Sol* H12 and becomes reconciled at *La* H24. If reconciled *Mi* H96 *doesn't* receive the shock of H24, it will turn active and start to descend.

My discovery was this new movement. I realized that the Enneagram started to be something that now could explain the Food

Diagram. Ouspensky quotes Gurdjieff as saying that in what he calls the "law of Heptaparaparshinokh," which is the law of seven, or the law of octaves, there are two shocks: the shocks at *Mi-Fa* and *Si-Do*. And in *Beelzebub*, there is an additional or third shock mentioned. My view of the shocks in the Enneagram is in figure 3.

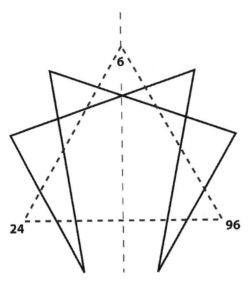

(Fig. 3 Shocks)

This is the basic Enneagram movement towards evolution. Starting at the pinnacle of the triangle, H6; the right side, H96; the left side H24: these shocks are necessary to complete triads or not to complete them, to turn the triad from a reconciled note to a passive note or to maintain ascension. All movement in the Enneagram is triadic. We think a shock is accidental. What would it mean, if every shock were identifiable? Well, it is, and it's governed by laws. It's not accidental. What I've discovered is that the triangle represents the law of shocks. (See fig. 3.)

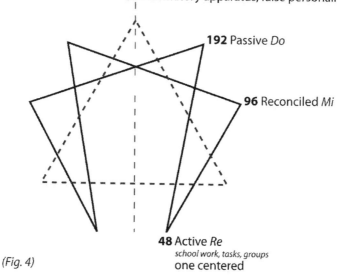

192 Passive *Do*

96 Reconciled *Mi*

48 Active *Re*
school work, tasks, groups
one centered

(Fig. 4)

All hydrogens have physical properties and psychological properties. These properties can change depending on the Enneagram. Consider, for example, the Enneagram I developed called Enneagram of Change of State. Almost everyone on the planet is deeply asleep, mechanical, a machine. I pegged H384 as formatory apparatus—or what was called false personality by Gurdjieff. *H384 is not in the Enneagram*; it is complete imagination and doesn't fit in this Enneagram. However, if H96 is brought to H384, it would reconcile at H192, bringing you into the Enneagram; H96 is essence. When someone asked Gurdjieff on what level of life did the Way begin, he said, "On no level. The Way begins on a level that is higher than life." But there is a staircase between life and the Way, a preparatory work. In order to get from your state of sleep into the Enneagram, you need to bring the idea of the Work, the feeling of the Work, the energy of the Work. Or nature could help you do it on a life level: take a walk in the woods; try to save the whales; do something essential. If you could bring H96 to H384, the struggle could bring you to H192, the impression of postures and tensions, the holding of the breath, small anxieties—things like that. If you reach H192 in this way, it is *active* H192. But with the correct struggle it can become *passive* H192, and

201

then it's possible to meet active H48 and be reconciled at H96. (See fig. 4.)

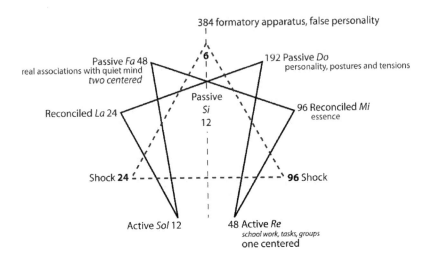

(Fig. 5)

For H384 to move to H192 it needs a triadic energy from H96. What I've discovered is that this triangle reflects a movement; that movement makes it possible for H96 to be brought to H384, bringing you into the Enneagram. What do the hydrogens mean? This is the way of expressing the connection between vibration and materiality. In speaking about the density of vibrations, Gurdjieff said, "Hydrogen 3072 is iron; H1536 is wood; H768 is food for man; H384 is water; H192 is air; and H96 is 'animal magnetism or rarified gasses.'" As the vibrational values become finer, numbers get smaller. In fact, he gave a wonderful definition of hydrogen 96. Someone asked him, "What exactly is hydrogen 96?" He said, "Well, if you have a lot of it, fleas don't bite you." What I've discovered about this finer energy is that people are attracted to it, especially people who don't have it. When you have it, better things become available. You attract finer things to yourself. Negative emotions interfere with it; they take it away. But H96 is a very special energy.

Gurdjieff spoke about H48 as being the energy of the head; the body works with H24; the emotions work with H12. He said these are not measurable by modern science. In putting these hydrogens into the Enneagram, I saw the triadic *movement* of the triangles in the Enneagram.

I'm usually not in the Enneagram. I normally live in the band of *active* H384 to *active* H192 which must to be turned passive in order to move further into the Enneagram. The chief characteristic of *passive Do* H192 is self-observation. If I remember my aim, if I remember what I wish, my task, what do I find? I experience my tensions and postures, sense the holding of my breath. And if you can be present at those moments when you come back to yourself, you will see I'm not *passive/receptive*: my personality is *active*; all my energy is going out. *How do I get to passive Do?* At that moment I see the lie that I live. I turn towards active H48, which is methods of work, the attempt to sense my body or do my weekly task by bringing my attention out of the path of least resistance. This new struggle at *that* moment can keep me from going back to H384. To bring *active* H48 to *active* H192, for example, I put my attention on my arm or leg or face: a struggle ensues between these *two active forces*, active personality, H192; and active H48, methods of work. The result of this friction between two active forces is that active H192 turns to passive/receptive H192.

All of these are idealized numbers: H96 is really an evolutionary movement from H192 to H96. Entrance into the Enneagram begins with active *Re* H48, the methods of work, being brought to passive *Do* H192, and the result is reconciled *Mi* H96, essence. Everything would stop there and begin to descend quickly unless I bring the shock of H24 from the left side of the Enneagram to reconciled *Mi* H96.

How do we move along the Enneagram? It takes conscious labor and intentional suffering. And that's exactly what it is, except in the Enneagram we need to know how that would relate to my attention. How will I get this triadic movement to be reconciled at *Mi* H96? It takes an expansion of the attention that includes two forces, passive *Do* H192 and active *Re* H48. The main characteristic of H48 is self-remembering; the characteristic of passive H192 is self-observation. These two efforts need to happen *simultaneously*! If I can look *out* and *in* and at the same time, expanding my attention to another center, I will move along the Enneagram. It is through an expansion of attention that includes active and passive, both forces together, a divided attention. (See fig. 4 again.) If the result of this struggle is maintained for a sufficient length of time, these two forces reconcile at *Mi* H96. The main characteristic of reconciled *Mi* H96 is this energy moving by itself; there's no additional effort required.

Now, how do we go further? Reconciled H96 needs a shock according to the Enneagram. That shock comes from bringing H24 from the left side of the Enneagram to reconciled *Mi* H96 on the right. (See fig. 5 again.) Here H24 represents the energy of the body, a real resonance in me. For the first years in the Work, it's very difficult to know that because I haven't gone through the octave of postures and tensions to relaxation often enough, so I can't sense H24. Maybe I experienced H24 when I was a child. But as we get older, we develop inner tensions, and we carry more and more baggage. In the Work, if we struggle, we shed baggage; that's how conscious labor and intentional suffering pays off in time. Finer hydrogens are very expensive. You have to pay whatever the price. You have to "buy" them. Some people are not willing to spend or pay the price. You pay the price, not with money, but with effort and the struggle against ego, the struggle with not being satisfied at a point where you're receiving something, like a better state, for example. Let's say at reconciled H96 you're accumulating finer energies. At that moment you have to *not* value that; you have to become passive to this new movement, which then makes you uncomfortable. When you open your attention to include both active and passive, it's very uncomfortable. I see that I'm not unified. *This is intentional suffering.* That resonance resounds within me and produces a shock that brings me to passive *Fa* H48 *on the left side of the Enneagram*, which I call "real associations to quiet mind." (See fig. 5 again.) Passive *Fa* H48 is very important to understand because at the moment I'm sensing my body, I'm connected with a resonance, an energy, that's whole. At this point I add the energy of the mind, and I become two-centered.

Expansion of consciousness isn't the expansion of a center; it's the adding of centers, the relationship between centers. H96 to H48 is *associations*—not formatory associations, but higher-quality associations on the journey to quiet mind. At quiet mind, I can take in real impressions. Even at H96 I can start to take in *some* impressions. In the Work we learn that our identification with thoughts is "bad." We have a long education in this struggle with formatory thoughts and bad associations. Now, I need to sense my body in order to get out of my head. At passive *Fa* H48 on the left side of the Enneagram I *need* my head. These new associations aren't negative: if I can maintain a connection with this resonance of H24, I will move to passive *Fa* 48, or quiet mind. The danger of these associations is that I can easily become identified. Why? I'm thinking to myself, "I'm having my best thoughts." How many times have you meditated and better solutions to problems come? I remember once somebody came to the group and said, "I have my best thoughts during my sitting." But if I become identified with them, I lose the resonance. I go backwards, towards H384 and out of the Enneagram. If I don't *maintain* that resonance, I must go back to formatory thoughts. And that happens time and time again. I must learn to recognize the differences between the formatory thinking of H384 and thinking in the band H96 to H48. The problem we face is that when we're sensing ourselves, when we're sitting or we're innerly working with an active attention, and we come to a state in which there *is* more sensation, we must realize that these new associations may *not* be formatory and they may be necessary. Now, if I could be *not identified* with these thoughts in my ordinary way but sense the energy and at the same time maintain both sensations and associations, my mind will quiet. Quiet mind is alien to the way we live. It's a new way of thinking. In a state of quiet mind a new energy can appear which is very high. But we don't maintain quiet mind long enough to go further. We're addicted to a *busy* mind. We associate associations with ordinary life, with many I's, so we never come to a place, or value a place, in which we are completely quiet. In that new quiet place I could become a receiver rather than a transmitter; and at

H48, if I'm a receiver I could receive H12, which is a very, very high energy spiritually.

I developed two primary Enneagrams. The first is the Enneagram of the Change of State and the second is the Enneagram of the Level of Being. The Enneagram of Change of State deals with short-term inner changes—things that could take place in a moment, an hour, or a day. One will then go back to what could be called the center of gravity of one's normal state. Your level of being is determined by your central hydrogen. Everybody has a certain level of being, or central hydrogen. Let's say my level of being is H192, but to evolve to H96 it moves through 191, 190, 189, 188, right on up. There are no jumps. Every step is earned. The Enneagram of Change of Being takes place over years, decades, or a lifetime. These two Enneagrams may have the same notations at the same points but in change of state one can *move*—through an influence, through struggle, through meditation, through the impacts of life, a very strong shock, or a teacher, or doing Movements. We've all experienced change of *state*. You can move through this Enneagram quickly, but you will always come back to your basic central hydrogen, your level of being. To change your level of being takes *consistent* work over many years.

The Enneagram shows you exactly what hydrogen or food you need at the various shocks and intervals in order to change your level of being. It shows you the exact effort you need to go further, and if you can know the exact effort and could identify the exact hydrogen of the shock, you could save a lot of unnecessary time. Necessary time cannot be saved, I say this again and again, but unnecessary time can be saved.

We feel this would be the right place to stop the description of Jerry's Enneagram. We have a great deal of material on this subject and the further description of working on the left side of the Enneagram, which will be the subject of a future book.

"There is another kind of vibration that comes from being centered, so we've got to start being more serious about sensation, about being a vessel for sensation of another kind; it's like one energy fits into the other energy."

14

As described in Jerry's Enneagram

THE ENERGY OF HYDROGEN 24

14.01 Q: You mention a special energy which you call H24. Could you elaborate more about that? At different times you have said it's "the gold that makes gold," the energy that accelerates transformation, and that this is the way to approach or arrive at first conscious shock.

J.B.: What I refer to as H24 is a vibration that is too fine to be perceived by our personality. As you become more aware of yourself, more sensitive, it's possible to perceive even higher levels of energy too. We are so used to the movement of the contents of the centers. We need to begin with a void. In order to really explain this, I have to go back to the origin of my experience with this energy, before I gave it labels.

When we first come to the Work and for a long time we struggle, trying to be present, to have one center observing another center so that there can be more impartial observation. I call this the "triad of interference."

Mme. de Salzmann brought us tasks on participation and brought work on centering, and one worked at that for a long time. In connecting to this place in us that is almost like the source of instinctive energy, the center that instinctive energy circulates around is not like an ordinary center. It's not the mind, not the feelings, not the ordinary body; it's "home space" that has a different kind of substance. Many times Mme. de Salzmann called it "void" or "emptiness," and many religions or spiritual ways say you must come to silence, to emptiness. This is a place that has no content, but by struggling with it, and failing, and struggling, and occasionally having a shift of attention, you get results. Mme. de Salzmann brought many, many exercises to do this in the sitting, and many ways to bring this into life. In my trying to be connected with this very subtle resonance, subtle and so light that it would seem meaningless, it would come and be gone quickly because the results would take over. As I struggled in my quiet work, I made the connection and I started to follow what I call a hum. I found this hum only came in very special circumstances, in special conditions of work, a few times in life. I couldn't really produce it at will, on my own. In preparing for taking groups I found out that being connected with this hum gave me great insights into what each person was saying. But it was only for moments, and I started to become very hungry for it, thirsty for the hum. I started to want this vibration in me all the time.

Around this time I had suggested to some of the older people that I knew in the Work that we get together to discuss things from the work we had been given, and during those meetings I would be trying to connect with this vibration. I found that it was a little bit easier for this resonance to appear when working with others. I often organized more than one meeting in a day, and sometimes I would have meetings from 4:30 to 10:30 or 11:00 at night. After a period of time, instead of having this hum for three minutes during the meeting, I would have it for ten minutes, and later, for fifteen minutes. I spent at least two days a week like this, and I started to judge my work from the point of view of this connection. If the hum, that resonance, wasn't there, I felt I wasn't really present. I devised new meetings or other work activities, and wherever I went I was searching for this vibration. After a year or two I could have it for almost a whole meeting. I would even sense the way people breathed. I attribute the quieting of the mind to this resonance. I could be without a thought, taking in impressions on this resonance. Sometimes, on some mornings, at the exact moment of awakening it seemed to become strong. And its effect of the resonance on my mind was interesting; through it I found a different substance in me. One day, while taking in impressions, I tried to be in every cell of my body, sensing the impact on the whole, and that vivified this resonance, which I now refer to as H24. I believe in the Enneagram it would be the succeeding higher H24; it's always active, what Gurdjieff calls the "Omnipresent-always-active-Okidanokh." I remembered something from the Philokalia, which I'll paraphrase: one needs to take an impression as an impact on the whole body. I think it is the special energy that Mme. de Salzmann was talking about when she would say, "It's not vivid enough; we have to vivify it." I felt that was very much the case with this vibration.

I found the work on centering helped a great deal in the beginning. It supported a place in me where the resonance could appear. If I could maintain this resonance for a period of time, I started to be without associations; then this resonance combined with the energy of the mind, and I would start to find a balance between mind and body. But then I started to notice that I had no feeling. It seemed these energies tuned towards each other, and there was a call to the emotions but there was no emotional energy available at the right level for this new tuning. Where is the *real* emotion at that level? My negative emotions, my ordinary emotions, were meaningless in this work. There was something about the lack of real emotion, of not having the right energy. I started to suffer greatly in this feeling of being emotionally dead. I remember going to Mme. de Salzmann and asking her about the energy, this hum, this resonance. She looked at me and said: "This is what Mr. Gurdjieff brought to us." She also said, "Now, you have to suffer this. You are suffering, right?" I said, "I am suffering terribly." She said, "Well, maybe this is the beginning of what could be conscience, and that's the level that you need. But that is very difficult." So I went on this way. And truthfully, faith, love, and hope never came into the picture. I am not sure conscience ever came. I don't think at the time I could have borne it. Later, at a certain point, I could bear it. The suffering was lessened and a different kind of feeling appeared, though I never felt that it was the right feeling for reconciliation to unity.

I remember going from 4:30 to 11:00 at night, two or three nights a week, working almost every moment because that energy had captivated me. Not emotionally: It wasn't like I loved it. I knew there was something about it that I needed. I was being fed! If I had a stronger pull to the monastic life, I would have gone somewhere to just sit in this resonance; that is all you have to do. At some meetings you have to talk, at some you don't. It didn't matter. I started to have fewer and fewer associations. There were times when I could be without associations at all. I remember driving two and a half hours up to my summer home in Mt. Pleasant without a thought, just watching with this vibration.

At one point an enormous fear and panic started to take over. I started to feel I was dying. What was happening really was my conceptual I *was* dying because it's based on associations, dreams, and formatory thinking, and now I was without it. I struggled to face this panic and fear. I was determined to stay rooted in this energy and not give in to associations. I found that the chasm of fear was deep but not wide; I got over it very quickly, and that surprised me. And then I was able not only to not feel fear, but to feel being. You don't need to associate; you don't need to dream. And the result of this work is that your mind becomes much more agile. You're able to see cause and effect more easily.

I realized personality cannot perceive this vibration; to perceive it, you have to be more essential. It was in the moments that I became more essential that I started to sense this energy. I realized that this vibration had to be brought to my groups. I could bring tasks; I could keep people in front of a struggle; but I had to bring that vibration. In my groups people were brought out of their personality into essence more often when I had this energy. If it wasn't strong during my day and people in groups came with their strong personalities, I found I was pulled too. I would have to sense a part of myself strongly to resist the pull .

I evolved a theory of the nontriadic relationship of energies as a basis for accelerated transformation and change. In the scale of hydrogens that I use for the Enneagram, H192 is personality; H96 is essence; H48 includes methods of the work; and then there's the succeeding higher, H24, which is not triadically related to H192. I realized that this energy was H24 and that personality could not perceive H24. H24 brings you to the first conscious shock, remembering yourself in front of an impression. It's an energy that you can carry. It's not based so much on attention because the resonance doesn't leave so quickly. Ordinarily, if you sense your foot and you lose your attention, you're gone, but if the sensation is deep enough, when you lose your attention the deeper sensation pulls you back to the moment. If you're connected with the resonance of H24, it's the same except it's wider, more whole. I believe that it's the only energy that I have come across, in me, that is in every cell of the body. It doesn't have its area in the way the mind has the head, the sexual center has its erogenous zones, and emotions have the solar plexus.

To help clarify this, my wife Sharon and I once went to a party to meet someone in the Work and later go out with them. I suddenly connected with H24, and it stayed with me. So I was vibrating with this energy when I was greeted by the hostess, whom I didn't know. I told her I was a friend of so-and-so. She said, "Oh wonderful, why don't you come in." After a little while, I noticed the hostess stayed with us, even though her friends came over and invite her to join them. She said no and she stayed with us, talking and talking. We didn't really have much in common with her.

Sometime later she had another party and she invited us back. I went, and when I saw her I said, "Let me ask you about that first night I came, you stayed by us. I mean, you never left even though people were calling you, and it seemed the wrong thing for a hostess to do." She said, "You know, you're right, I am very surprised at this. But, you know, I couldn't leave you." I said, "Why?" She said, "I don't know. I felt like I was a child again." I went on to understand that it's all in the vibrations, but this was later when it became obvious.

I started to see not only how the triadic relationship of these energies worked but also how H24, when it's vivified, can dissolve personality. One day, in my gallery I was concentrating on this resonance, and I was able to maintain it. In life it's very hard to maintain, but this day I woke up. I was talking to a person in the gallery, still connected to this vibration, and suddenly this person stepped on my pet corn, and I saw a tremendous emotional reaction jump out of me but I was still vibrating. And the reaction to this

212

person came out without its posture, without the mental attitudes that support it. It was just like being with Mme. de Salzmann, the way I would see a feature through her being a mirror for me. At that moment I saw that I had developed this reaction as a child, that this was a typical part of my personality, that I reacted this way all the time, and I saw that the future would be always the same; and then, suddenly it was gone, never to come back again! Personality disappears when this energy is present, like in a sitting. It won't reveal itself. It's only in life that my pet corn would be stepped on. Suddenly, the genius of why Gurdjieff insisted that work in life was necessary became apparent to me.

These features must come out in life; they're geared for life. But we can't maintain the energy and attention long enough to see them with any clarity. If I were sensing my right leg and I jump up, the sensation in my right leg would be gone and I would become identified with the jumping up. But if I had this resonance H24, I wouldn't become as identified. I began to see how being identified with everything affected my life and that I didn't have to be that way! Later I started to see more and more. Eventually, a feature would come out, not as dramatic as that, but life would provide a certain irritation, certain impatience, and a certain way of dealing with people. It was an effective, very quick way of eliminating it. While I was in that vibration anything I saw was gone. It even zapped my associations, my formatory thoughts. Not that I don't ever have them now; certainly, one reverts a certain amount, but I don't live with them in the same way. I remember especially long periods of clarity of thought. In this state of clarity I had a new understanding of the Enneagram. I became receptive to flashes of knowledge that I don't know how I knew. That's part one. There are a number of parts about H24.

As I became a little more essential in my life, H24 started to become perceptible to me. I worked on myself and made progress, dropped many postures and tensions. However, I got caught up in the results—emotional and mental clarity, a sense of well-being. But those results were already the descent, the pouring out of the energy. I went from somebody who for years did things poorly to someone who took pride in every detail; so it was this impression of doing something really well, more consciously, with hydrogen 24 that allowed me to develop an inner authority that maybe certain people in the Work saw as ego. I certainly didn't feel it was ego; in fact it was *the giving up of ego*! I didn't have to consider; my actions were for the right reasons, going against the things that put one in a state of considering.

Once it was decided to have an exhibition of Nathalie Etievan's paintings in New York. Nathalie is Mme. de Salzmann's daughter, and she was a painter from what they call the school of the naïve; in America, they call it primitive art. Leading up to the show, I decided to visit the gallery to see how it was coming along. I owned a New York gallery and was a professional in this field. I was horrified. Everything about the display was wrong. The way it came off the wall was wrong. But I started to feel this energy of H24 and I said, "I'm taking over." I didn't care if the people responsible objected or not. I said, "Look, I'm a professional. I'm taking over this show. We're going to have to rehang the whole show, and we're changing all the rules." And we did. I rehung the whole show with them, showing them exactly the principles of how to hang it, and even how to deal with people who think they might wish to buy something. It takes someone who understands this principle to help customers to buy, especially those with the most money, to eliminate the no: the science of selling.

The whole show sold out—every piece! At the end of the show Nathalie took all the people involved to dinner at the Russian Tea Room. I sat next to her, and we just talked about things in general. None of us were connected with her in groups. We just knew her and respected her. I remember that the vibration of H24 was very strong. It was shimmering in that room, in part because of the success of the show. I saw it clearly. There was no doubt anymore. And I saw that the tendency would be to have the energy pour out, but I stayed with the energy, and at the end of the evening, I still remember very vividly crossing 57th Street, and every step affirmed this energy. That was the first moment in which I clearly understood that the struggle and staying with H24 was more important than the result, such as a successful show. Up to that point I had been addicted to results.

Mme. de Salzmann used to say, "No energy stays alone; it either relates to a higher energy or a lower energy," and that certainly is the key to the law of Triamazikamno and the Enneagram. So I started to open up to the mind: I had a divided attention plus this vibration of hydrogen 24, and as the thoughts of personality started to be more and more exposed to this energy I would see them and try to maintain both together; and this had the effect of not only dissolving the associations but also lengthening the time that I could be *without* them. How can you be without associative thoughts? It's like losing your mind, and if one gives in to that fear, that identification, one stops working immediately. "Who am I?" What was the sense of I was lost, and this is where the panic begins. Instead of stopping work, I stayed in front of the panic; it's a chasm that may be deep but not wide. I brought hydrogen 24 to it, and the panic couldn't stand before this resonance. I was in a state where I enjoyed not thinking, not associating. I didn't know what thinking was. A new way of thinking began to appear. Later this all became part of the basis of my work on the Enneagram, in the sense of the effect it had on me, which enabled me to have what you would call no-mind, or quiet mind.

The next experience I want to speak about was more than about doing something well. It was connected to my greatest fear in the Work: that one day I would have to *answer* a question in front of Mme. de Salzmann. When Christopher Fremantle died I knew that Mme. de Salzmann was trying to understand who should work in front of groups. There was a big meeting of all groups together with their leaders. When I arrived, I heard Mme. de Salzmann say, "Have Brewster sit up with us." When I heard that a pang of fear went through me. The meeting went on; Mme. de Salzmann and Henri Tracol answered questions. At one point, someone asked a question and Mme. de Salzmann said, "Have Brewster answer that one." And my heart went in my mouth. As I looked inside I found nothing. The only thing I had was the ability to search for this vibration of hydrogen 24, what I had called the hum. But I'd learned to trust it and I decided I wasn't going to speak unless that vibration was in me.

I sat there, and time passed and it didn't come, and time passed. This is the loudest silence you could possibly imagine, and everybody in the group was looking at each other, and I was waiting. Finally, I started to sense the vibration so I started to speak. I said a sentence, and my voice went up, maybe an octave and I stopped. I realized that I had gone right to my head. I waited again, and the vibration came back very quickly and I started to speak again. I couldn't believe what I was saying. For a minute I thought maybe Mme. de Salzmann was a ventriloquist because this couldn't be coming out of me; this answer really was wisdom! I still remember the question and I still remember the answer.

The question was, "I've been struggling and working. My wish carried me all these years. Now I've come to an interval and my wish has disappeared."

I said, "Well, maybe your work, your wish, took you a certain distance on the path; don't regret that. But now you have to sacrifice your old wish. It won't take you further. You need to find a *new* wish. You're put into the unknown; you must really search, now, for what could take you further. There is a Buddhist story in which a man comes to a large river filled with crocodiles and strong currents. He sits and meditates. After he meditates he realizes he's got to build a raft that takes him across the river. After crossing, he sees he has to climb a large mountain and he has this dilemma: this raft helped him enormously; it took him across the river which would have stopped him. Now, does he try to climb the mountain carrying the boat or does he leave it behind? The raft is like your old wish. You must let it go and proceed." Much later, I was talking to Henri Tracol, and he said, "You remember that night that you spoke? We could see what happened. We could see how you spoke." The result of the meeting was that I kept my group. Mme. de Salzmann said, "You were the only one allowed to take their group alone," and I know it came from that answer and about answering a question in front of her.

H24 is an accelerated path to transformation. Later, Mme. de Salzmann came to my older group a number of times, and I never felt one iota of nervousness or fear again. That fear had dissolved. In fact, I know I even got a little too glib because Tracol came over to me once and said so. He said, "Look, I know you know what you're talking about, but you speak too glibly about it, too readily about it." He said, "It might be better to sometimes play a role. Sometimes you've got to make believe you're searching for the answer." It was wonderful of him that he told me that. It showed me that he cared. I wanted to think about what he said because it's really interesting, how to present it in a right way. I realized he was right because I *did know*. As people spoke, I'd be in this place, and I would know exactly what they were saying, and I'd know exactly what to say. And I *would* say it a little too quickly. Maybe that's where my fault is. I felt it came from experience, but I don't know. Maybe it *was* a fault that I didn't hesitate and play a role. I understood that there is something about changing the tempo, searching; sometimes I could do it, sometimes I couldn't.

What took place from having terrible jobs that I hated when I was younger . . . I was a dispatcher for a photographer for baby pictures, worked dispatching trucks, hating every job and being very bad at them but meanwhile going to Mendham, and later, Armonk. I felt the importance of second line of Work because I needed it desperately. And through it I learned how to function, how to do things really well, and I learned how to bring it into life. Second line of Work is really a bridge between the real, underlying work and life, so I was able to start having moments of feeling in life. I changed from someone who was not a very good worker to someone who could dedicate eighteen hours a day to accomplishing his tasks, and went from a basement frame shop in the Village to a Madison Avenue art gallery. It was a meteoric rise.

Through the years I had many experiences with H24. For instance, I was often very busy in my gallery on Madison Avenue. I didn't have much help and had to do most of the dealing and most of the selling because it's a very difficult thing to teach people to sell art. It was hectic and demanding every minute. I would go to the Foundation for a meeting with one of my groups, and I was usually rushed as I walked in, and there were times I didn't have five minutes before the meeting but figured, "Okay, the meeting will bring me to a state, I can work on myself there." When I had H24 in me I received

217

the impressions of myself in states coming directly from life. After a while I couldn't bear myself in a state of such unpreparedness. I became sensitive to it and no matter what happened at the gallery during the day, I would somehow make time before the meeting to stay connected—not because I wanted to, but because it was a necessity, because I couldn't bear the impression of seeing myself in such a mechanical state. Preparation supported my work in front of the group. I started to take in impressions in a new way. As people spoke, I could actually see the way they breathed, where the breath was coming from; I could see the state they were in and where their attention was. This was particularly interesting because I was just bringing centering to my oldest group.

Also, when I was rushing over to the Foundation, I often stopped at a hot dog vendor and ate on the way. It gave me some sustenance and I got to like them. One day I was preparing myself much earlier. And even though it was a little hectic, I was able to maintain a connection with H24 for a longer period. On my walk over to the Foundation I bought my usual hot dog, but this time I wasn't rushing; I was present. As I started to eat, I couldn't believe what I tasted! The impressions started to come in; I could taste every chemical, I think I even tasted the negative emotions of the guy who cooked the hot dog. I started to sense an aura of negativity around this hot dog. The taste became so atrocious that I couldn't eat a hot dog for a year because of the memory of that taste. Later I discovered a very good kosher hot dog at Papaya King.

Another H24 story: I was going to go on a five-day work period at Armonk. I had just moved my gallery from 79th Street to 57th Street, basing my whole business on a series of lithographs I was going to publish with Francisco Zùñiga. It would give me a phenomenal income and free me up because I was getting very busy with the Work. It was becoming difficult to be at the gallery all day long selling art and then meeting with people in the Work. The day before this work period I met with Zùñiga's son regarding the book about his father. The son was very difficult and was sabotaging deals that I had made with his father. Zùñiga himself had liked our progress, but I was changing something and the son flipped out, went through the roof! His final words were, "You will never work with my father again!" I also had a very close personal relationship with Zùñiga, and this could have been disastrous from the point of view of our relationship.

That evening, carrying this huge wound in my emotions, I drove to Armonk for the group work period. It was like somebody had stabbed me—a traumatic wound. I saw that my mind went to it every thirty seconds; I would think about the injustice, on and on and on. I realized something: I remembered that a reminding factor is a very important thing. I decided that every single time I saw myself thinking about this, I would center myself, and try to come back to the energy of H24. At first it was very difficult, but I started to do it; I was coming back to being centered. Armonk was the right atmosphere where people could work, but instead of the work period consisting of me sitting in a group discussing an idea of Gurdjieff's and then returning to my thinking about what happened with Zùñiga, I was centering. Slowly this wound started to heal, started to go away, and after about two or three days, I was innerly free of the whole situation. It was a miracle. A few weeks later Zùñiga's son came to me and said, "My father decided that you're going to be the sole distributor of his lithographs." This experience showed me a connection with how you use the negative things in life as reminding factors.

At one point, a strange thing started to happen. I thought I was losing this connection with H24. I thought it was an interval and tried many things to bridge it. It was as if this higher energy wasn't separate from me anymore, wasn't as distinct as it had been. But I finally started to understand that it didn't leave me: it had joined me, and this long struggle had produced a reconciliation; it became a part of how I lived, a change in the fabric of my being. I needed to begin a search for a new active *Do* of the next octave. The old personality of Jerry Brewster didn't exist anymore. I had opened to a new value system.

For instance, I worked with Leonora Carrington as her art dealer and was invited to her party at which the really big lights of the literary and the artistic world would be. Christopher Fremantle was also invited; he was a good friend of Leonora's. The party turned out to be on the same night that we had a group meeting. It was a small group, the beginning of what is now my older group. As Christopher and I were walking over to the party, he said, "I know Leonora personally. I must stay for the party. Could you take the group alone tonight?" I said, "Certainly, I'd be glad to. Of course I'll take the group." It turned out that the party wasn't just for Leonora. It was for me as well, as her dealer. It was actually to celebrate her opening at the Brewster Gallery. I was one of the luminaries, so to speak, at the party. There were speeches being made, people talking, drinking and toasting, "Here's to Leonora! Here's to Jerry!" I could only stay twenty minutes because I had to get to the group. I remember walking out, walking down Park Avenue, and something stunned me: I had absolutely no regrets at leaving the party. There was no place that I wanted to be more than with that group. At that time I still had a hunger and a thirst for fame. Where were those I's that valued being lionized at a party of socialites and the top people in the literary and art worlds? I realized that something had changed in the fabric of my being. I had seen this in people like Mme. de Salzmann, Michel de Salzmann, Mme. de Hartmann, Henri Tracol, but you can't fake it. No regrets leaving and, as I said, actually looking forward to the group meeting: that change was the action of H24 on my being.

Another factor of H24: I would find that if I woke up in the morning without a thought *at the exact second* I woke up, if I went directly to the vibration of H24 that I knew was there, it would become supercharged. I would then have five or ten minutes in which the energy would be like a train going through me. I turned away from the results; the energy was more important than the result, how to stay with this energy. That's all you need and I felt that's all I wanted. I've said in the past, I think that's the real meaning of the alchemist's statement that to make gold it takes some gold. I believe they were working with vibrations and energies of a very fine nature. It takes some H24 to produce H24. Only then, if you activate the first conscious shock, does it bring you to reconciled *La* H24.

BIOGRAPHICAL NOTE

Jerry Brewster was born Joseph Jacob Blaustein on October 1, 1928, and passed on February 12, 2009, at age 80. He grew up in meager conditions in the South Bronx. His father died at a young age. He was raised by his working mother and two aunts, and made New York City his home. In his later years he suffered from both diabetes and MDS (a form of leukemia). In 1953 a friend introduced Jerry to the Gurdjieff Work. Jerry was a jazz saxophonist at the time, caught up in the 1950s excitement of bebop.

After leaving the music industry and taking a series of menial jobs he became an expert at framing and gilding, opened a picture framing shop, and later became an art dealer opening the Brewster Gallery located on upper Madison Avenue and then on West 57th Street. Jerry also became exclusive agent for the prints of Mexican artist Francisco Zùñiga, and later an art publisher, authoring *Zùñiga: The Complete Graphics, 1972–1984.*

At the Gurdjieff Foundation he took Movements with Alfred and Lise Etievan, and Jessmin Howarth. He participated in a Movements demonstration at Carnegie Hall in the early 1960s.

Christopher Fremantle instructed Jerry, Lillian Firestone, and Jim Wyckoff to lead groups. In the late 1960s, Jerry assisted Fremantle with several groups in New York. His groups were an offshoot of that effort.

Through experiencing the effects of conscious efforts on his own business success, Jerry strongly urged members of his groups to use their inner work in life, to provide the battlefield on which to overcome the difficulties of remembering oneself and bringing that struggle. He had a gift of both remembering and inventing tasks and reminding factors; this was in addition to providing conditions for working with others through readings, study, and the exchange of ideas and projects, and the design and production of craft items that were sold to help raise money to fund Mme. de Salzmann's film *Meetings with Remarkable Men*. Jerry believed the Work was a science. He often said that as evidenced by the successes in his own life, "the Work works."

Jerry worked with many people who worked directly with Mr. Gurdjieff. He traveled regularly to Gordes, France, to work with M. Tracol; and to Chandolin, Switzerland, to work with Dr. Michel de Salzmann; and to Paris to work with Mme. de Salzmann.

Jerry was a spellbinder at giving talks on the ideas of Gurdjieff. He traveled to Connecticut, Florida, and Arizona to give talks on the Work. He once gave a public lecture at the Morikami Museum in Del Ray Beach, Florida, that attracted a number of new people to groups there. There were also weekly talks and discussions on the ideas of Gurdjieff, which he felt were very important, and he used to demonstrate the significance and practicality of inner work by responding to experiences brought by members of the groups.

If he were asked his own most important contribution, Jerry probably would have said that it would be his new ideas on and more complete formulation of the Enneagram, verified by his own experience and his reading of *Beelzebub* and *In Search of the Miraculous*. He shared this in depth with his groups for many years starting in 1989.

Jerry always stated that the Work must continue to develop and evolve, to develop people to carry on the teaching. Quoting Mme. de Salzmann, "I cannot do it, but without me, it cannot be done."

Index

enlighten(ed)(ment) 51, 64, 93, 94, 124

Enneagram 2, 3, 5, 14, 24, 32, 47-49, 51, 52, 54, 60, 68, 69, 71, 74, 79, 86, 87, 92, 93, 95, 96, 105, 110, 111, 113, 115, 116, 153, 154, 156, 160, 165, 192-194, 196-206, 208, 210, 211, 213, 215, 222

Essen(ce)(tial) 6, 11, 12, 14, 17, 20, 38, 45, 47, 48, 49, 51- 53, 61, 67, 74, 80, 81, 85, 87, 88, 98-101, 104-106, 111, 113, 118, 127, 129, 132, 133, 138-140, 161, 190, 194-196, 201, 203, 211, 213

and personality 98

essence profit 18, 19, 32, 45, 47, 85, 96, 99, 116

evolve(s)(ed)(ing) evolution(ary) 18, 45, 47, 48, 50- 52, 69, 74, 76, 79, 81, 82, 85, 86, 93, 97, 102, 103, 110-110, 112, 117-119, 126, 145, 165, 196, 197, 199, 200, 203, 206, 211, 222

exercise(s)(ed)(ing) 8, 10-13, 21- 24, 27, 33, 37, 41, 49, 65, 67, 70, 71, 86, 110, 111, 122, 134, 144, 147, 148, 160, 178, 179, 209

exist(s)(ence) 6, 9, 12, 27, 28, 32, 38, 51-53, 58, 59, 65, 66, 69, 71, 72, 76, 80, 85, 86, 88, 100, 106, 107, 111, 116, 117,123, 127, 132, 140-142, 144, 148, 156, 160, 164, 219

expansion, expanded attention 9-11, 14, 23, 27, 28, 72, 91, 113, 122, 123, 141, 144, 203-205

experience(s)(ed)(ing) 2, 12, 14, 18, 21, 23, 25, 26, 28, 29, 31, 33, 41, 49, 54, 57, 58, 64, 65, 67, 68, 72, 82, 87, 90, 92, 93, 96, 99, 101, 104, 106-110, 116, 120, 122, 123, 129, 130, 132, 133, 142, 145, 146, 152, 161-164, 176, 178, 181, 182, 191-194, 203, 204, 206, 208, 215, 217, 219, 221, 222

experiment(ation) 19, 20, 33, 53, 96, 113, 165, 179

extraordinary(iness) 26, 39, 40, 50, 58, 76, 80, 88, 89, 109, 141, 148, 153, 154, 161, 165, 169-172, 181, 182, 186, 187, 191

F

fail(ed)(ure)(ing) 18, 40, 58, 69, 70, 80, 92, 107, 209

faith 28, 101, 122, 134, 195, 210

fakir(s) 19, 77, 148, 149

false personality 6, 47, 90, 104, 201

fate 116

fear(s) 49, 54, 57, 60, 68, 161, 211, 215, 216

feature(s) 18, 20, 34, 35, 67, 87, 89, 103, 128, 156, 160, 191, 213 (see chief feature)

feel(ing)(s) 5, 13, 14, 23, 26, 27, 29, 31-35, 37, 38, 44, 47-49, 51, 52, 66, 68-77, 80-82, 88, 90, 92, 94, 100, 102, 107, 109, 110, 114, 116, 118, 120-123, 129, 132-134, 139, 141, 142, 145, 146, 148, 149, 151, 152, 155-157, 159, 160, 167, 173, 177, 188-191, 195, 198, 201, 209- 211, 214, 217

first conscious shock 5, 22, 32, 69, 98-100, 208, 211, 220

food(s) 7, 30, 34, 66, 98-100, 127, 202, 206

food diagram 8, 69, 86, 126, 127, 194, 200

force(s) 10-12, 14, 17, 18, 21, 22, 24, 27, 28, 38, 40, 41, 46, 50-53, 58-60, 62, 65, 66, 68, 69, 71, 74-76, 79-82, 85-87, 91-93, 97, 98, 100, 108. 110-113, 115, 117-119, 122, 123, 141, 154, 160, 196, 203, 204

form(s) 7, 32, 41, 43, 73, 74, 92, 117, 126, 165, 181, 186, 198

formatory 7, 28, 47, 68, 101, 121, 141, 142, 192, 194, 201, 205, 211, 213

formula 79, 196

formulate(ed)(ion) 31, 107, 148, 161, 163, 165, 222

Fourth Way 2, 42, 77, 99, 147-149

free(ing)(d)(r) 8, 14, 17, 20, 26, 32, 37, 38, 48, 52, 56-58, 60, 67, 82, 91, 94, 117, 121, 129, 135, 139, 159, 184, 191, 196, 219

freedom 48, 195

Fremantle, Christopher 70, 98,157, 158,174,

179, 180, 215, 219, 221

friction 12, 111, 203

function(s) 41, 69, 71, 102, 114, 217

G.

gnostic 38

God 7, 11, 14, 26, 31, 32, 40, 45, 46, 53, 61, 64, 67, 69, 81, 87, 94, 99, 100, 105-107, 110, 111, 115, 124, 153

go(ing) against 13, 35, 36, 40, 41, 51, 53, 58-60, 62, 76, 77, 84, 90, 100, 113, 146, 147, 157, 180, 204, 214

gospel(s) the 38, 95

group leader(s) 2, 18, 19, 31, 35, 36, 38-41, 75, 77, 90, 104, 110, 113, 118, 158, 164, 166, 170, 175, 178, 179, 215

group work 5, 6, 17-19, 21, 22, 24, 25, 33-37, 40-42, 60, 70, 73, 77, 83, 88, 94, 97, 105, 106, 116, 119, 127, 128, 158, 159, 164, 167, 168, 172, 176, 178-181, 205, 216, 219, 222

guided sittings 20-22, 24-26, 156

Gurdjieff, G.I. 5-7, 9, 11, 12, 19-23, 26, 29, 31, 35, 37, 40-42, 45, 46, 49-51, 57, 58, 60-62, 64, 65, 68, 69, 71-73, 75, 79, 85, 87, 88. 90, 93-95, 98-100, 102-112, 115, 121, 123, 126, 127, 129, 133, 135, 138, 139, 142, 145-147, 151-153, 159, 164-167, 169, 172, 174, 176, 179-181, 186,187, 194, 196,-198, 200-202, 210, 213

H

habit (s) 11, 72, 84, 85, 135

habitual(ly)53, 74, 100, 121, 132, 135, 139, 160

harmonius circle 117

harmon(y)(ious)(ize) 91, 100, 122

Hasnamuss 40,

Heaven, Kingdom of 95,

Higher body(ies) 22, 65, 66, 99, 103, 109, 126, 128, 146

higher center(s) 7, 20, 29, 33, 41, 49, 52, 64, 68 103-105, 142, 146, 147, 161, 162, 196

higher energy(ies), vibration(s), force(s) 7, 11, 14, 18, 22, 24, 33, 34, 41, 47, 48, 50, 52, 60, 64, 65, 71, 72, 74, 75, 79-82, 86-89, 92, 94- 97, 99, 100, 103-110, 116, 118, 122, 141, 160, 189, 195, 197, 199, 208, 210, 215, 219

higher level(s) state(s) 5, 42, 64, 73, 81, 88, 89, 96, 97, 99, 105. 145, 147, 166, 201

note(s) of the octave 49, 66, 71, 74, 91, 96, 115, 117, 122, 160, 200

nothingness 66, 160

not knowing 108, 142

O

obey 9, 99

objective(ly)(ity) 6, 18, 39, 41, 42, 47, 51, 53, 75, 87- 90, 101, 102, 122, 159, 181, 193

objective conscience 49, 89

objective consciousness 102, 104, 105

observe(s)(ed) see self-observation 6, 33, 53, 66, 77, 86, 88, 89, 98, 99, 114, 128, 139, 143, 144, 160, 161, 208

obstacle(s) 14, 41, 90, 91, 160, 161

octave(s) 35, 40, 50, 51, 66, 67, 69, 71, 72, 74, 76, 80, 85, 86, 91, 92, 96, 97, 102, 104, 105, 107, 108, 110, 113, 115, 117-119, 134, 145, 160, 193-195, 197, 200, 204, 216, 219

open(s)(ed)(ing) to 8, 10-12, 14, 20, 23, 24, 27, 29, 31-33, 49, 50, 52, 66, 71-74, 76, 80-82, 96, 98, 100, 103, 107, 109, 111, 113, 118, 133, 134, 139, 141-143, 146, 147, 152, 156, 161, 165, 179, 190, 194, 204, 215, 219

ordinary 9, 10, 20, 22, 23, 30, 47, 61, 64, 66-68, 71, 82, 140, 146, 198, 205, 208, 210, 212

organic 13, 92, 191

organic life on earth 50

P

pain(ful) 70, 102, 104, 106, 108, 178, 195

participate(ion)(ing)19, 20, 24, 32, 33, 54, 75, 95, 97, 113, 114, 116, 139, 150, 157, 158, 160, 167, 179, 208

passive *Do* 20, 48, 50, 51, 52-54, 74, 81, 85-87, 111, 112, 197, 199, 202, 203

passive(ly) 10, 11, 24, 47, 48, 50, 51, 53, 74, 81, 82, 87, 93, 197, 199, 200, 204, 205

passive (force) 10-12, 50, 69, 76, 79, 91, 100, 111, 113, 115, 119, 196

passive/receptive 12, 24, 51, 52, 74, 80, 86, 112, 203

path(s) 22, 26, 41, 54, 68, 76, 77, 103, 216, 216

path of least resistance 9, 10, 18, 21, 27, 48, 65, 80, 85, 86, 100, 107, 115, 139, 145, 147, 152, 159, 199, 203

pay(s)(ment) 47, 140, 204

pendulum(atic) 73,   74,

perceive(ed)/perception(able) 66, 90, 100, 160, 208, 211-213

permanent 'I' 5, 9, 31, 32, 47, 80, 103, 105, 141

personality(ies) 6, 7, 10-12, 14, 18, 19, 24, 26, 30, 32, 34, 36-38, 41, 44, 45, 47-54, 57, 61, 65, 67, 68, 74, 80-82, 85-87, 90, 93, 95-101, 104, 106, 110-113, 118, 122, 126-128, 132, 133, 135, 139, 140, 144, 156, 158-160, 168, 195, 196, 203, 208, 211-213, 215, 219

personality, false 6, 47, 90, 104, 201

personality('s) profit 18, 19, 32, 45, 47, 85, 96, 99, 116

photograph(s)(ic)16, 87, 173

physical center/body or energy 32, 62, 84, 105, 120, 121, 138, 142, 148, 152, 194, 195, 201